The
TIGHT BUDGET
COOKBOOK

Delicious & Nutritious Recipes

for the

Frugal Cook

edited by

Heidi Smalheiser

E & E Publishing
Sausalito, California

Published by
E & E Publishing,
a Registered Trade Name of
THE E & E GROUP LLC
1001 Bridgeway, No. 227
Sausalito, California 94965
U.S.A.
Website: www.EandEGroup.com/Publishing
Email: EandEGroup@EandEGroup.com

Printed in U.S.A.

DEDICATION

For
my mother,
Shirley Smalheiser,
whose
cooking,
cookbooks,
and
joie de vivre
are an inspiration.

acknowledgements

Recipes for this cookbook were contributed by Nutrition Educators associated with the following:

Arizona Nutrition Network
California Department of Health Services
California Health Department - Los Angeles County
Centers for Disease Control
Clemson University Division of Public Service & Agriculture
Contra Costa Health Services, Contra Costa County, California
Connecticut Departments of Public Health and Social Services
Cornell Cooperative Extension, Division of Nutritional Sciences Cornell University
Food and Health Communications, Inc.
Indian Health Service Division of Diabetes Treatment and Prevention
Iowa State University Extension
Johnson and Wales University and Rhode Island Department of Health WIC Program
Kansas Family Nutrition Program
Kansas State University Research and Extension
Kansas State University Cooperative Extension
Michigan Department of Community Health
Michigan State University Cooperative Extension Service
Missouri Nutrition Network
Montana State University Extension Service
National Cancer Institute
National Heart, Lung and Blood Institute
National Institutes of Health (NIH) and Food and Drug Administration (FDA)
Ohio State University Extension
Oregon State University Extension Service
Pennsylvania Nutrition Education Program
Quick and Healthy, 1995, Brenda Ponichtera, RD, ScaleDown Publishing, Inc.

Rutgers Cooperative Extension
University of California Cooperative Extension
University of Connecticut Cooperative Extension
University of Connecticut Family Nutrition Program
University of Hawaii at Manoa Cooperative Extension
University of Illinois Extension Service
University of Kentucky Cooperative Extension Service
University of Massachusetts Extension Nutrition
   Education Program
University of Minnesota Extension Service
University of Nebraska Cooperative Extension Service
University of Nevada Cooperative Extension
University of Rhode Island Cooperative Extension
University of Wisconsin Cooperative Extension Service
University of Wyoming Cooperative Extension
USDA Center for Nutrition Policy and Promotion
USDA Consumer and Marketing Service
USDA Food and Nutrition Service
USDA Food Distribution Program on Indian Reservations
USDA Team Nutrition
Utah State University Cooperative Extension
Virginia Cooperative Extension
Washington State University

CONTENTS

INTRODUCTION

If you want to save a lot of money on your grocery bills, yet still serve delicious and nutritious meals, this cookbook is for you!

All of the recipes in this book were contributed by Nutrition Educators with your needs in mind. You'll find breakfast dishes for as little as 4 cents per serving, and main dishes featuring meat for as little as 51 cents per serving.

With hundreds of recipes, you'll find everything from breakfast; main dishes with meat, poultry, fish and a section for vegetarians; side dishes, salads; snacks, soups and stews; breads and muffins; desserts; and sauces, condiments and dressings.

The ingredients used in the recipes are common and easy to find.

Detailed nutritional information is given per serving, including calories and the amount of fat, protein, carbohydrate, cholesterol and sodium.

And, equally important, the cost of each recipe and each serving is also provided. This cost information[1] reflects the national average

---

[1] Recipe costs are based on information provided by the USDA Economic Research Service, which was updated in July, 2008, based on food prices through December, 2007. This is the most recent information available from the USDA at the time of publication of this volume.

price of the ingredients. The actual prices that you will pay may be different, due to differences in locale and time of the year.

However, the cost information provided for each recipe and serving provides an excellent guideline when planning your meals to accommodate to your grocery budget.

Bon appétit!

FOOD SAFETY TIPS

Follow these ten steps to maintain a safe kitchen:

Step 1: Your Refrigerator

Keep your refrigerator at 40°F (4°C) or less. A temperature of 40°F or less is important because it slows the growth of most bacteria. The fewer bacteria there are, the less likely you are to get sick from them.

Step 2: Perishable Foods

Refrigerate cooked, perishable food as soon as possible within two hours after cooking. Date leftovers so they can be used within two to three days. If in doubt, throw it out!

Step 3: Kitchen Dishcloths and Sponges

Sanitize your kitchen dishcloths and sponges regularly. Wash with a solution of one teaspoon chlorine bleach to one quart water, or use a commercial sanitizing agent, following product directions.

Many cooks use dishcloths or sponges to mop up areas where they have worked with uncooked meat and then reuse the cloth or sponge in other kitchen areas after minimal rinsing.

A contaminated dishcloth can house millions of bacteria after a few hours. Consider using paper towels to clean up and then throw them away immediately.

Step 4: Cutting Boards

Wash your cutting board with soap and hot water after each use.

Never allow raw meat, poultry, and fish to come in contact with other foods. Washing with only a damp cloth will not remove bacteria.

Periodically washing in a bleach solution is the best way to prevent bacteria from remaining on your cutting board.

Step 5: Cooking Meats

Cook ground beef, red meats and poultry products to a safe internal temperature. Use a meat thermometer.

Cooking food, including ground meat patties, to an internal temperature of at least 160°F (72°C) usually protects against foodborne illness.

Ground beef can be contaminated with potentially dangerous E. coli bacteria.

The US Department of Agriculture Food Safety and Inspection Service (FSIS) advises consumers to **use a meat thermometer** when cooking hamburger and not rely on the internal color of the meat to be sure it is safe to eat. Research indicates that some ground meat may turn prematurely brown before a safe internal temperature of 160°F (72°C) is reached.

Step 6: Mixes Containing Egg

Don't eat raw or lightly cooked eggs.

Many older cookbooks have recipes for ice cream, mayonnaise, eggnog and some desserts that call for raw eggs. These recipes are no longer recommended because of the risk of Salmonella. The commercial versions of these products are made with pasteurized eggs (eggs that have been sufficiently heated to kill bacteria) and are not a food hazard.

Remember—this means no sampling of cake batters and cookie dough before they are baked!

Step 7: Kitchen Counters

Clean kitchen counters and other surfaces that come in contact with food with hot water and detergent or a solution of bleach and water.

Bleach and commercial cleaning agents are best for getting rid of pathogens. Hot water and detergent do a good job, too, but may not kill all strains of bacteria. Keep sponges and dishcloths clean because, when wet, these materials harbor bacteria and may encourage their growth.

Step 8: Washing Dishes by Hand

Allow dishes and utensils to air-dry in order to eliminate re-contamination from hands or towels.

When washing dishes by hand, it's best to wash them all within two hours—before bacteria can begin to form.

Step 9: Washing Hands

Wash hands with soap and warm water immediately after handling raw meat, poultry, or fish.

Wash for at least 20 seconds before and after handling food, especially raw meat. If you have an infection or cut on your hands, wear rubber or plastic gloves.

Step 10: Defrosting Meats

Defrost meat, poultry and fish products in the refrigerator, microwave oven, or cold water that is changed every 30 minutes.

Follow package directions for thawing foods in the microwave. Cook microwave-defrosted food immediately after thawing.

Changing water every 30 minutes when thawing foods in cold water ensures that the food is kept cold, an important factor for slowing bacterial growth on the outside while inner areas are still thawing.

Rise and Shine Cobbler

Serving Size: 3/4 cup
Yield: 4 servings

Ingredients:

1 cup canned, drained and sliced peaches
1 cup canned, drained and sliced pear halves
6 pitted prunes - each cut in half
1/4 teaspoon vanilla extract
1 orange
1 cup granola, low-fat

Instructions:

1. In a large microwave-safe bowl, mix peaches, pears, prunes, and vanilla extract.

2. Rub an orange against a grater to remove 1 teaspoon of the orange peel. Then, cut the orange in half and squeeze 1/4 cup orange juice. Add orange peel and juice to fruit mixture. Stir.

3. Top with granola.

4. Microwave on high for 5 minutes. Let stand for 2 minutes.

5. Spoon into 4 bowls and serve warm.

Per serving: 280 calories, 1 g fat, 3 g protein, 67 g carbohydrate, 0 mg cholesterol, 60 mg sodium

Cost: Per Recipe: $ 2.14; Per Serving: $ 0.54

Breakfast Burrito

Serving Size: 1 burrito
Yield: 4 servings

Ingredients:

4 large eggs
2 Tablespoons frozen corn
1 Tablespoon 1% milk
2 Tablespoons diced green peppers
1/4 cup minced onions
1 Tablespoon diced fresh tomatoes
1 teaspoon mustard
1/4 teaspoon granulated garlic
1/4 teaspoon hot pepper sauce (optional)
4 - 8 inch flour tortillas
1/4 cup canned salsa

Instructions:

1. Preheat oven to 350 degrees.

2. In a large mixing bowl, blend the eggs, corn, milk, green peppers, onions, tomatoes, mustard, garlic, hot pepper sauce, and salt for 1 minute until eggs are smooth.

3. Pour egg mixture into a lightly oiled 9x9x2 inch baking dish and cover with foil.

4. Bake for 20-25 minutes until eggs are set and thoroughly cooked.

5. Wrap tortillas in plastic and microwave for 20 seconds until warm. Be careful when unwrapping the tortillas. The steam can be hot.

6. Cut baked egg mixture into 4 equal pieces and roll 1 piece of cooked egg in each tortilla. Serve each burrito topped with 2 Tablespoons of salsa.

Per serving: 250 calories, 9 g fat, 11 g protein, 31 g carbohydrate, 210 mg cholesterol, 600 mg sodium

Cost: Per Recipe: $ 1.33; Per Serving: $ 0.33

Fruit and Yogurt Breakfast Shake

Serving Size: 1/2 of recipe
Yield: 2 servings

Ingredients:

1 medium, very ripe, peeled banana
3/4 cup pineapple juice
1/2 cup yogurt, low-fat vanilla-flavored
1/2 cup strawberries, remove stems and rinse

Instructions:

1. Blend banana with pineapple juice, yogurt and strawberries in a blender.

2. Blend until smooth.

3. Divide shake between 2 glasses and serve immediately.

Per serving: 160 calories, 1 g fat, 4 g protein, 37 g carbohydrate, 5 mg cholesterol, 45 mg sodium

Cost: Per Recipe: $ 1.03; Per Serving: $ 0.52

Banana Pancakes with Apple Topping

Serving Size: 1/6 of recipe
Yield: 6 servings

Ingredients:

2 eggs
1 1/2 cups 1% milk
1 Tablespoon honey*
3 Tablespoon oil
3/4 cup whole wheat flour
3/4 cup all purpose flour
2 teaspoons baking powder
2 bananas
Apple Topping:
3 apples
3 Tablespoons sugar
1 teaspoon cinnamon
1/4 cup water

Instructions:

1. Beat eggs. Beat in milk, honey and oil.

2. Add flours and baking powder.

3. Slice bananas and add to mixture.

4. Coat a large, non-stick frying pan or griddle with non-stick cooking spray. Warm the pan over medium heat for 2 minutes.

5. Spoon 1/4 cup of the batter onto the heated griddle for each pancake (adjust more or less depending on pancake size).

6. Cook until the tops are bubbly and the pancakes are dry around the edges. Flip and cook for 2-3 minutes or until golden on both sides. Place pancakes on a platter and keep warm.

7. Repeat steps 5 and 6 until batter has been used, using more non-stick cooking spray as needed.

Apple Topping:
1. Wash apples, remove cores, and slice thinly with peel still on.

2. Combine apples with the sugar, cinnamon, and water.

3. Cook in skillet for 10 minutes and spoon on top of pancakes.

***Note:** Infants 12 months and under should NOT be given honey.

Per serving: 330 calories, 10 g fat, 9 g protein, 55 g carbohydrate, 75 mg cholesterol, 220 mg sodium

Cost: Per Recipe: $ 2.45; Per Serving: $ 0.41

Apple Slice Pancakes

Serving Size: 2 pancakes
Yield: 6 servings

Ingredients:

1 Granny Smith apple
1 1/4 cup any type pancake mix
1/2 teaspoon cinnamon
1 egg
2 teaspoons canola oil
1 cup low-fat milk

Instructions:

1. Lightly coat a griddle or skillet with cooking spray and heat over medium heat.

2. Peel, core and thinly slice apple into rings.

3. In a large mixing bowl, combine ingredients for pancake batter. Stir until ingredients are evenly moist. (Small lumps are ok! Over-mixing makes pancakes tough.)

4. For each pancake, place apple ring on griddle and pour about 1/4 cup batter over apple ring, starting in the center and covering the apple.

5. Cook until bubbles appear. Turn and cook other side until lightly brown.

Notes: To test the griddle to see if it is hot, sprinkle it with a few drops of water. When the drops sizzle and dance, you are ready to cook! The easiest way to pour the batter onto the hot griddle is to use a 1/4 cup measuring cup for each pancake. If the first pancake is too brown, lower the heat.

Per serving: 160 calories, 4 g fat, 5 g protein, 24 g carbohydrate, 45 mg cholesterol, 360 mg sodium

Cost: Per Recipe: $ 1.24; Per Serving: $ 0.21

Pumpkin Pancakes

Serving Size: 1 pancake
Yield: 12 servings

Ingredients:

2 cups flour
2 Tablespoons brown sugar
1 Tablespoon baking powder
1 1/4 teaspoon pumpkin pie spice*
1 teaspoon salt
1 egg
1/2 cup canned pumpkin
1 3/4 cup milk, low-fat
2 Tablespoons vegetable oil

Instructions:

1. Combine flour, brown sugar, baking powder, pumpkin pie spice and salt in a large mixing bowl.

2. In a medium bowl, combine egg, canned pumpkin, milk and vegetable oil, mixing well.

3. Add wet ingredients to flour mixture, stirring just until moist. Batter may be lumpy. (For thinner batter, add more milk).

4. Lightly coat a griddle or skillet with cooking spray and heat on medium. Using a 1/4 cup measure, pour batter onto hot griddle. (Pan is "hot" when a drop of water "dances.") Cook until bubbles begin to burst, then flip pancakes and cook until golden brown, 1 1/2 to 2 1/2 minutes. Repeat with remaining batter. Makes about 1 dozen 3 1/2 inch pancakes.

***Note:** You can substitute 3/4 teaspoon cinnamon, 1/4 teaspoon nutmeg and 1/8 teaspoon each of ginger and cloves for the pumpkin pie spice.

Per serving: 130 calories, 3.5 g fat, 4 g protein, 21 g carbohydrate, 20 mg cholesterol, 340 mg sodium

Cost: Per Recipe: $ 1.13; Per Serving: $ 0.09

Cornmeal Pancakes

Serving Size: 1 pancake
Yield: 20 servings

Ingredients:

2 cups cornmeal
1 teaspoon baking powder
1/2 teaspoon soda
1 teaspoon salt
1 teaspoon sugar
2 Tablespoons margarine or butter
1 3/4 boiling water
1 cup evaporated milk
1 Tablespoon vinegar
1 egg

Instructions:

1. Measure, place in a bowl and mix cornmeal, baking powder, salt, and sugar.

2. Measure fat (butter or margarine), and add to cornmeal mixture. Bring water to a boil. Measure 1 3/4 cups boiling water, and add to cornmeal mixture. Beat until well mixed.

3. Measure evaporated milk, and pour into a small bowl. Measure vinegar, and stir into evaporated milk. Stir milk and vinegar mixture into cornmeal mixture. Beat to mix well. Beat in egg. Makes batter for 20 medium-size pancakes.

4. Grease griddle or fry pan lightly, then heat. (If electric fry pan is used, preheat it to 380 degrees.) Pan is "hot" when a drop of water "dances."

5. Pour batter onto griddle or fry pan. Use about 3 Tablespoons batter for each pancake. A 1/4 cup measure is handy to use for pouring. Stir the batter up from the bottom now and then to keep it well mixed. Cook until top is covered with bubbles and the bottom is brown. Loosen edges of each pancake all around. Turn pancakes over and brown other side.

Main Dishes—Meat

Baked Pork Chops, 50
Beef Pot Roast, 33
Carne Adobado (Spiced Pork,
    42
Cheesy Swiss Steak, 38
Enchilada Rice, 46
Garden Chili, 44
Honey Mustard Pork Chops,
    35
Manly Muffin Meat Loaf, 41
Marinated Beef, 45
Misickquatash (Indian
    Succotash), 39
Pineapple Pork, 48
Quick Skillet Lasagna, 40
Sensational Six-Layer Dinner,
    43
Slow-Cook Barbecue, 47
Spinach and Meat Cakes, 34
Stove-Top Tamale Pie, 36

Beef Pot Roast

Serving Size: 3 ounces
Yield: 8 servings

Ingredients:

1/2 cup chopped onion
2 cups water
2 1/2 pounds boneless beef chuck roast
2 cups hot water
1 beef bouillon cube
1 Tablespoon orange juice
1/4 teaspoon allspice
1/8 teaspoon pepper

Instructions:

1. In a small bowl, put the bouillon cube in 2 cups hot water. Stir it until the bouillon cube dissolves. This will make 2 cups of beef broth.

2. In a medium bowl, stir together the broth, orange juice, allspice, and pepper.

3. Peel and chop the onion, to make 1/2 cup chopped onion.

4. Put 2 tablespoons water in the skillet. Heat on medium.

5. Put the onion in the skillet. Simmer it until tender.

6. Add the roast to the skillet. Brown it on all sides.

7. Pour the broth mix over the meat in the skillet.

8. Cover and simmer for 2 hours.

Per serving: 360 calories, 26 g fat, 27 g protein, 1 g carbohydrate, 95 mg cholesterol, 200 mg sodium

Cost: Per Recipe: $ 6.35; Per Serving: $ 0.79

Spinach and Meat Cakes

Serving Size: 2 meat cakes
Yield: 6 servings

Ingredients:

1 pound ground beef, or turkey, 7% fat (93% lean)
2 bunches spinach - washed and cut into pieces (may
substitute a 1-pound bag of frozen chopped spinach,
thawed and well drained)
1/2 small finely chopped onion
2 minced garlic cloves
1/2 teaspoon salt
black pepper to taste
3 cups cooked brown rice

Instructions:

1. Preheat frying pan (no oil).

2. Combine all ingredients except brown rice in a large
mixing bowl. Mix well.

3. Form mixture into 12 small balls. Place in frying pan
and flatten into patties using a spatula.

4. Cook over medium heat until cooked on both sides.

5. Serve over brown rice.

Per serving: 270 calories, 9 g fat, 21 g protein, 27 g
carbohydrate, 50 mg cholesterol, 340 mg sodium

Cost: Per Recipe: $ 5.63; Per Serving: $ 0.94

Honey Mustard Pork Chops

Serving Size: 1 pork chop
Yield: 4 servings

Ingredients:

4 top loin pork chops
1/3 cup orange juice
1 Tablespoon soy sauce
2 Tablespoons honey mustard

Instructions:

1. Put the pork chops in the large non-stick skillet.

2. Cook over medium-high heat to brown one side of the pork chops.

3. Use the spatula to turn the chops.

4. Add the rest of the ingredients and stir.

5. Cover the pan and lower the heat.

6. Simmer for 6 to 8 minutes until chops are done.

Note:
Pork chops are done when they reach an internal temperature of 160 degrees, and when the inside of each chop is a light shade of pink.

Per serving: 230 calories, 11 g fat, 24 g protein, 6 g carbohydrate, 65 mg cholesterol, 360 mg sodium

Cost: Per Recipe: $ 2.06; Per Serving: $ 0.51

Stove-Top Tamale Pie

Serving Size: 1/4 of recipe
Yield: 4 servings

Ingredients:

Quick Chili:
1/2 pound ground beef, lean
1 can (15 1/2 ounce) kidney beans - drain and save liquid
1/3 cup bean liquid
1 cup canned tomato puree
1 Tablespoon minced onion
1 1/2 Tablespoons chili powder

Tamale Pie:
8 ounces canned, not drained whole kernel corn
1/2 cup yellow cornmeal
dash salt
1 1/4 cups cold water
1/8 teaspoon chili powder

Instructions:

Prepare Chili:

1. Cook beef in hot skillet until lightly browned. Drain off fat.

2. Stir in remaining ingredients. Bring to a boil.

3. Reduce heat, cover, and simmer 10 minutes.

Prepare Tamale Pie:

1. Place chili in a 10-inch skillet. Stir in corn. Heat thoroughly.

2. As chili heats, mix cornmeal and salt with water in a sauce pan. Cook over medium heat, stirring constantly until thickened, about 2 minutes.

3. Spread cornmeal mixture over hot chili to form a crust. Sprinkle with chili powder.

4. Cover and cook over low heat, with lid slightly ajar, until topping is set, about 10 minutes.

Per serving: 340 calories, 8 g fat, 21 g protein, 46 g carbohydrate, 35 mg cholesterol, 650 mg sodium

Cost: Per Recipe: $ 2.87; Per Serving: $ 0.72

Cheesy Swiss Steak

Serving Size: 1/8 of recipe
Yield: 8 servings

Ingredients:

2 pounds beef round roast (1-inch thick)
1/4 cup flour
1/2 teaspoon salt
2 chopped carrots
1/4 cup chopped onion
1/2 teaspoon Worcestershire sauce
1 can (8 ounces) tomato sauce
1/2 cup American cheese, shredded

Instructions:

1. Cut the beef roast into 4 pieces.

2. In a small bowl, mix the flour and salt.

3. Dip each piece of meat into the mix of flour and salt. Coat it on all sides with the mix.

4. Put the meat in a crock pot.

5. Add the chopped carrots and onion.

6. Add the Worcestershire sauce and tomato sauce.

7. Cover and cook on low for 8-10 hours, OR on high for 4-5 hours.

8. Just before serving, sprinkle the cheese on top.

Per serving: 210 calories, 7 g fat, 29 g protein, 7 g carbohydrate, 65 mg cholesterol, 470 mg sodium

Cost: Per Recipe: $ 8.11; Per Serving: $ 1.01

Misickquatash (Indian Succotash)

Serving Size: 1/6 of recipe
Yield: 6 servings

Ingredients:

1 cup lean ground beef
1 cup frozen lima beans - cooked and drained
1 can (15 1/2 ounce) corn - drained
1 can (15 1/2 ounce) tomatoes - broken up
1/4 teaspoon salt
1/4 teaspoon pepper
1/8 teaspoon nutmeg

Instructions:

1. Brown ground beef in pan.

2. Add remaining ingredients except nutmeg. Cover and simmer 5 minutes until thoroughly heated.

3. Sprinkle with nutmeg before serving.

Per serving: 160 calories, 3.5 g fat, 10 g protein, 19 g carbohydrate, 20 mg cholesterol, 420 mg sodium

Cost: Per Recipe: $ 3.14; Per Serving: $ 0.52

Quick Skillet Lasagna

Serving Size: 1 cup
Yield: 7 servings

Ingredients:

1/2 cup chopped onion
1/2 pound ground beef
1 can (16 ounce) tomatoes
1 can (6 ounce) tomato paste
1 Tablespoon fresh parsley (optional)
1 1/2 cups water
1 teaspoon garlic powder (optional)
2 cups egg noodles
3/4 cup cottage cheese, low-fat
1/4 cup Parmesan cheese

Instructions:

1. Chop onion. Cook beef and onion, in the frying pan until beef is brown and onion is tender. Drain off excess fat.

2. Add tomatoes, tomato paste, parsley, water, and garlic powder to the beef mixture. Bring to a boil and simmer until sauce is thick, about 25 minutes.

3. Cook noodles in the saucepan according to package directions. Drain.

4. Add cooked, drained noodles to the beef mixture. Stir to prevent sticking.

5. Mix cheeses and drop by spoonfuls into the frying pan.

6. Cover and heat over low heat about 5 minutes.

Per serving: 200 calories, 6 g fat, 15 g protein, 23 g carbohydrate, 40 mg cholesterol, 440 mg sodium

Cost: Per Recipe: $ 3.81; Per Serving: $ 0.54

Manly Muffin Meat Loaf

Serving Size: 2 muffins
Yield: 6 servings

Ingredients:

1 egg
1/2 cup non-fat milk
3/4 cup oats
1 pound lean ground beef
3 Tablespoons chopped onion
1/2 teaspoon salt
1/2 cup grated cheese (any variety)

Instructions:

1. Preheat oven to 350 degrees.

2. Combine all ingredients and mix well.

3. Spoon mixture into greased muffin cups.

4. Bake for 1 hour, or until temperature in center of meat loaf is 160 degrees.

5. Cool slightly before removing from muffin cups.

Notes: Combine meat loaf ingredients until well mixed, but don't over mix; too much mixing can make a meat loaf tough.

Safety Tip: Cook your meat loaves to 160 degrees. Use a meat thermometer to test the temperature. You will know that your loaves will be completely and safely cooked without being dried out from overheating.

Per serving: 230 calories, 12 g fat, 21 g protein, 9 g carbohydrate, 95 mg cholesterol, 330 mg sodium

Cost: Per Recipe: $ 3.56; Per Serving: $ 0.59

Carne Adobado (Spiced Pork)

Serving Size: 1/12 of recipe
Yield: 12 servings

Ingredients:

2 cups red chili puree or 12 tablespoons chili powder
3 pounds fresh lean pork
2 teaspoons salt
1 Tablespoon oregano
2 mashed garlic cloves

Instructions:

1. Cut pork into strips.

2. Mix other ingredients, add to pork strips, and let stand in refrigerator for 24 hours.

3. Cut meat into cubes and brown in small amounts in oil. Add chili sauce and simmer one hour more.

4. To serve, add more fresh chili sauce and cook until tender.

Per serving: 190 calories, 9 g fat, 23 g protein, 5 g carbohydrate, 75 mg cholesterol, 550 mg sodium

Cost: Per Recipe: $ 8.38; Per Serving: $ 0.70

Sensational Six-Layer Dinner

Serving Size: 1/6 of recipe
Yield: 6 servings

Ingredients:

2 - 3 medium sliced potatoes
2 cups sliced carrots
1/4 teaspoon black pepper
1/2 cup sliced onion
1 pound browned and drained ground beef
1 1/2 cups green beans
1 can tomato soup

Instructions:

1. Lightly oil or spray baking dish with cooking spray.

2. Layer ingredients in order given. Cover.

3. Bake at 350 degree for 45 minutes or until tender and thoroughly heated.

4. Uncover and bake 15 more minutes.

Note: For variation, use peas or corn instead of green beans. Use your favorite cream soup instead of tomato soup.

Per serving: 230 calories, 6 g fat, 25 g protein, 17 g carbohydrate, 65 mg cholesterol, 580 mg sodium

Cost: Per Recipe: $ 5.10; Per Serving: $ 0.85

Garden Chili

Serving Size: 1/4 of recipe
Yield: 4 servings

Ingredients:

3/4 pound ground beef
1/2 cup chopped green pepper
1/2 large chopped onion
1/2 cup chopped celery
2/3 cup canned, drained and rinsed, kidney beans
1/2 cup sweet corn
8 ounces tomato sauce
1 cup chopped fresh tomatoes
dash black pepper
1/2 teaspoon garlic powder
2 teaspoons chili powder

Instructions:

1. Place ground beef in a skillet sprayed with non-stick cooking spray. Brown meat over medium-high heat until it is no longer pink, stirring occasionally to break it into pieces. Drain fat and blot meat with paper towels. Transfer beef into a colander and rinse with very hot water to further remove fat.

2. Add green pepper, onion, and celery. Cook until softened.

3. Add beans, corn, tomato sauce, chopped tomatoes, pepper, garlic and chili powder.

4. Cook mixture over low heat for 20 minutes.

5. Serve hot in bowls. Or serve as a dip with baked tortilla chips or on a bun.

Per serving: 250 calories, 9 g fat, 22 g protein, 22 g carbohydrate, 55 mg cholesterol, 530 mg sodium

Cost: Per Recipe: $ 3.99; Per Serving: $ 1.00

Marinated Beef

Serving Size: 1/4 of recipe
Yield: 4 servings

Ingredients:

12 ounces beef round steak
1 garlic clove
2 Tablespoons lemon juice
4 Tablespoons vegetable oil
1/2 teaspoon salt
1/2 teaspoon black pepper

Instructions:

1. Using a cutting board and sharp knife, cut round steak across the grain into thin strips about 1/2 inch wide and 2 to 3 inches long.

2. In a medium glass mixing bowl, combine garlic, lemon juice, 2 Tablespoons of vegetable oil, salt and pepper.

3. Add beef strips and stir to coat with the oil mixture (marinade sauce). Cover bowl with plastic wrap and refrigerate for about 2 hours.

4. In a medium skillet over medium-high heat, heat 2 Tablespoons of the oil for 1-2 minutes until hot.

5. Drain marinade from beef. Put beef in skillet, stir and cook for 5 to 7 minutes or until meat is thoroughly browned.

Per serving: 240 calories, 17 g fat, 20 g protein, 1 g carbohydrate, 45 mg cholesterol, 200 mg sodium

Cost: Per Recipe: $ 2.83; Per Serving: $ 0.71

Enchilada Rice

Serving Size: 1/6 of recipe
Yield: 6 servings

Ingredients:

1 pound lean ground beef or other ground meat
1/2 cup chopped onions or 1 Tbsp onion powder
1 can (14 ounce) whole corn or any canned vegetable, drained
4 Tablespoon dry taco seasoning mix or dry enchilada sauce
2 cups rice, cooked
1/2 cup grated cheese
1/2 cup sliced mushrooms, olives or any favorite vegetable (optional)

Instructions:

1. Cook meat and onion until onion juices are clear.

2. Drain juice and fat from cooked meat and onions.

3. Add corn, taco seasoning, and rice.

4. Simmer for 10 minutes.

5. Add grated cheese to top; cover and let set for 5 minutes.

Per serving: 240 calories, 4.5 g fat, 20 g protein, 30 g carbohydrate, 40 mg cholesterol, 540 mg sodium

Cost: Per Recipe: $ 4.65; Per Serving: $ 0.78

Slow-Cook Barbecue

Serving Size: 1/5 of recipe
Yield: 5 servings

Ingredients:

1 1/2 pound, boneless, 1 1/2 inches thick chuck steak
1 peeled and minced garlic clove
1/4 cup wine-vinegar
1 Tablespoon brown sugar
2 Tablespoons Worcestershire-sauce
1/2 cup ketchup
1 teaspoon salt (optional)
1 teaspoon dry or prepared mustard
1/4 teaspoon black pepper

Instructions:

1. Cut the beef on a diagonal, across the grain into slices 1 inch wide and place in a slow cooker.

2. Combine the remaining ingredients and pour over the meat.

3. Mix the meat and sauce together.

4. Cover and cook on low for 3 to 5 hours.

5. Serve on toasted hamburger buns with a mixed green salad.

Per serving: 310 calories, 17 g fat, 27 g protein, 11 g carbohydrate, 70 mg cholesterol, 390 mg sodium

Cost: Per Recipe: $ 4.81; Per Serving: $ 0.96

Pineapple Pork

Serving Size: 3 ounces
Yield: 4 servings

Ingredients:

1 medium green pepper, cut into strips
4 boneless pork chops (about 1 pound)
1/8 teaspoon salt
1 Tablespoon vegetable oil
1 can (8-ounce) pineapple chunks, undrained
1/4 teaspoon ginger
1/4 teaspoon cinnamon

Instructions:

1. Cut the green pepper into strips.

2. Heat the oil in a large skillet.

3. Place pork chops on the heated skillet. Sprinkle the salt on top.

4. Cook the pork for 5 minutes on low heat on each side.

5. The pork should lose its pink color when it's cooked enough.

6. Remove the cooked pork from the skillet. Place it in a serving dish.

7. Put the green pepper slices in the skillet.

8. Stir the in pineapple chunks with their juice.

9. Stir in the ginger and cinnamon.

10. Simmer for about 3-5 minutes.

11. Spoon the pineapple mixture over cooked pork.

Note: Serve with cooked rice.

Per serving: 270 calories, 14 g fat, 24 g protein, 9 g carbohydrate, 65 mg cholesterol, 140 mg sodium

Cost: Per Recipe: $ 4.56; Per Serving: $ 1.14

Baked Pork Chops

Serving Size: 1/6 of recipe
Yield: 6 servings

Ingredients:

6 pork chops, lean center-cut, 1/2-inch thick
1 medium thinly sliced onion
1/2 cup chopped green pepper
1/2 cup chopped red pepper
1/8 teaspoon black pepper
1/4 teaspoon salt
fresh parsley for garnish

Instructions:

1. Preheat oven to 375 degrees.

2. Trim fat from pork chops. Place chops in a 13x9-inch baking pan.

3. Spread onion and peppers on top of chops. Sprinkle with pepper and salt. Refrigerate for 1 hour.

4. Cover pan and bake 30 minutes.

5. Uncover, turn chops, and continue baking for an additional 15 minutes or until no pink remains. Garnish with fresh parsley.

Per serving: 160 calories, 9 g fat, 17 g protein, 4 g carbohydrate, 55 mg cholesterol, 150 mg sodium

Cost: Per Recipe: $ 5.30; Per Serving: $ 0.88

Main DISHES—CHICKEN & TURKEY

Crispy Oven-Fried Chicken

Serving Size: 1/2 breast or 2 small drumsticks
Yield: 6 servings

Ingredients:

1/2 cup nonfat milk or buttermilk
1 teaspoon poultry seasoning
1 cup cornflakes, crumbled
1 1/2 Tablespoons onion powder
1 1/2 Tablespoons garlic powder
2 teaspoons black pepper
2 teaspoons dried crushed hot pepper
1 teaspoon ground ginger
8 (4 breasts and 4 drumsticks) chicken pieces, skinless
a few shakes of paprika
1 teaspoon vegetable oil to grease baking pan

Instructions:

1. Preheat oven to 350 degrees.

2. Add 1/2 teaspoon of poultry seasoning to milk.

3. Combine all other spices with cornflake crumbs and place in a plastic bag.

4. Wash chicken and pat dry. Dip chicken into milk, shake to remove excess, then quickly shake in bag with seasoning and crumbs.

5. Refrigerate for 1 hour.

6. Remove from refrigerator and sprinkle lightly with paprika for color.

7. Evenly space chicken on greased baking pan.

8. Cover with aluminum foil and bake for 40 minutes.

9. Remove foil and continue baking for an additional 30 to 40 minutes or until the meat can be easily pulled away form the bone with a fork. The drumsticks may require less baking time than the breasts. Crumbs will

form a crispy "skin." (Do not turn chicken during baking.)

Per serving: 180 calories, 3.5 g fat, 28 g protein, 9 g carbohydrate, 80 mg cholesterol, 135 mg sodium

Cost: Per Recipe: $ 6.01; Per Serving: $ 1.00

Chicken and Dumplings

Serving Size: 1/2 of recipe
Yield: 2 servings

Ingredients:

2 Tablespoons all purpose flour
2 Tablespoons water
1 cup chicken broth
1 cup chicken, cooked and diced
1/4 teaspoon salt
dash black pepper
Dumplings:
1/3 cup all purpose flour
1/2 teaspoon baking powder
1/4 teaspoon salt
2 Tablespoons non-fat milk

Instructions:

1. Mix 2 tablespoons flour and water in a pan until smooth.

2. Slowly stir in broth.

3. Cook over medium heat until thickened.

4. Add chicken, salt and pepper.

Make Dumplings:

5. Combine 1/3 cup flour, baking powder, and salt in a small bowl. Stir in milk until dough forms.

6. Drop dumpling dough from a Tablespoon onto gently boiling chicken mixture, making 4 dumplings.

7. Cover pan tightly and cook slowly for 15 minutes without lifting the lid.

Per serving: 290 calories, 8 g fat, 28 g protein, 24 g carbohydrate, 65 mg cholesterol, 1560 mg sodium

Cost: Per Recipe: $ 1.41; Per Serving: $ 0.71

Chicken Cacciatore

Serving Size: 1/4 of recipe
Yield: 4 servings

Ingredients:

1 chopped onion
1 cup canned tomatoes
1/2 cup tomato sauce
1/8 teaspoon garlic powder
1 teaspoon oregano
1/8 teaspoon pepper
4 pieces chicken, skin removed (thighs, breasts, or legs)

Instructions:

1. Peel and chop the onion.

2. Put the chopped onion in a saucepan.

3. Add the tomatoes, tomato sauce, garlic powder, oregano, and pepper.

4. Simmer on low heat for 3 minutes.

5. Wash the chicken inside and out with clean water. Remove the skin.

6. Add the chicken to the sauce pan.

7. Cover the pan.

8. Cook over low heat for about 1 hour until the chicken is tender.

Per serving: 210 calories, 8 g fat, 24 g protein, 11 g carbohydrate, 75 mg cholesterol, 320 mg sodium

Cost: Per Recipe: $ 3.14; Per Serving: $ 0.78

Hawaiian Chicken

Serving Size: 1/5 of recipe
Yield: 5 servings

Ingredients:

1 teaspoon oil or margarine
2 1/2 pounds chicken, boneless skinless
1/4 teaspoon salt
1/8 teaspoon pepper
1 can (6 ounces) pineapple juice, frozen concentrate
2 cans (12 ounces) water

Instructions:

1. Defrost the pineapple juice.

2. Grease a large frying pan. Heat the pan on low. Put the chicken parts in the hot pan. Sprinkle with salt and pepper.

3. Cook until the chicken begins to brown.

4. Add the defrosted pineapple juice to the pan.

5. Swish the water in the can, and add it to the pan.

6. Cover and cook slowly, turning now and then, for 50 minutes or until the chicken is fork tender.

7. Put the chicken on a warm platter.

8. Skim the fat from the chicken juices in the pan.

9. Boil down the juices until they are slightly thickened (about 5 minutes).

10. Return the chicken to the pan. Reheat it for a few minutes.

Per serving: 340 calories, 8 g fat, 49 g protein, 16 g carbohydrate, 160 mg cholesterol, 300 mg sodium

Cost: Per Recipe: $ 7.84; Per Serving: $ 1.57

Oriental Rice

Serving Size: 1/4 of recipe
Yield: 4 servings

Ingredients:

1 Tablespoon vegetable oil
2 beaten eggs
3 1/2 cups rice, cooked
1 cup chicken breast, ham or pork, cooked and chopped
1 cup mixed vegetables, cooked and chopped
2 sliced green onions
soy sauce or hot sauce to taste (optional)

Instructions:

1. Heat pan. Add 1 teaspoon of oil. Add eggs and scramble.

2. Remove cooked eggs and set aside.

3. Add the rest of oil (2 teaspoons) to pan. Stir fry rice, breaking up lumps by pressing rice against pan.

4. Add leftover meat and/or vegetables. Stir-fry until heated.

5. Add green onions, reserved eggs and sauce to taste. Serve hot.

Per serving: 310 calories, 8 g fat, 17 g protein, 40 g carbohydrate, 135 mg cholesterol, 120 mg sodium

Cost: Per Recipe: $ 2.40; Per Serving: $ 0.60

Vegetable and Turkey Stir-Fry

Serving Size: 1/4 of recipe
Yield: 4 servings

Ingredients:

1 Tablespoon vegetable oil
1/2 teaspoon salt
2 thin slices ginger root - minced
1 peeled and minced garlic clove
1 - 2 cups turkey, cooked - cut into 1/2 inch cubes
1/2 teaspoon sugar
1 pound chopped vegetables, fresh or frozen
water (optional)

Instructions:

1. Heat fry pan. Add oil and heat on high temperature.

2. Add ginger, garlic, turkey and vegetables. Stir fry about 1 minute to coat with oil.

3. Adjust heat to prevent scorching. Add sugar. If vegetables are tender, stop cooking at this time.

4. If the vegetables are firm, add 1-2 tablespoons of water, cover and cook for 2 minutes or until tender.

5. Serve at once, or if you wish to add a gravy:

6. Mix the gravy ingredients well, pour over vegetables and turkey, cook for 30 seconds.

Per serving: 310 calories, 5 g fat, 49 g protein, 16 g carbohydrate, 125 mg cholesterol, 420 mg sodium

Cost: Per Recipe: $ 3.10; Per Serving: $ 0.77

Chicken and Broccoli Bake

Serving Size: 1/8 of recipe
Yield: 8 servings

Ingredients:

1 cup rice, uncooked
1 package (10 ounce) broccoli, frozen
3 cups chicken, cooked
2 Tablespoons margarine or butter
1/4 cup flour
2 cups chicken broth
1/4 cup Parmesan cheese (optional)

Instructions:

1. Cook rice in 2 cups of water.

2. Let broccoli thaw.

3. Chicken should be off the bone.

4. Melt butter in large sauce pan.

5. Add flour to melted margarine and stir. This will be lumpy.

6. Use broth from chicken you cooked or use canned chicken broth. Slowly add broth to margarine/flour. Stir to remove lumps and thicken.

7. Add cheese and stir.

8. Add rice, broccoli, and chicken. Stir.

9. Put in a casserole pan and bake at 350 degrees for 30 minutes or until thoroughly heated.

Per serving: 170 calories, 5 g fat, 19 g protein, 11 g carbohydrate, 45 mg cholesterol, 460 mg sodium

Cost: Per Recipe: $ 6.54; Per Serving: $ 0.82

Stuffed Green Peppers

Serving Size: 1 pepper
Yield: 4 servings

Ingredients:

4 large washed green peppers
1 pound turkey, ground
1 cup rice, uncooked
1/2 cup peeled and chopped onion
1 1/2 cups tomato sauce, no added salt
black pepper to taste

Instructions:

1. Cut around the stem of the green peppers. Remove the seeds and the pulpy part of the peppers.

2. Wash, and then cook green peppers in boiling water for five minutes. Drain well.

3. In saucepan, brown turkey. Add rice, onion, 1/2 cup tomato sauce and black pepper.

4. Stuff each pepper with the mixture and place in casserole dish.

5. Pour the remaining tomato sauce over the green peppers.

6. Cover and bake for 30 minutes at 350 degrees.

Per serving: 410 calories, 10 g fat, 26 g protein, 53 g carbohydrate, 90 mg cholesterol, 125 mg sodium

Cost: Per Recipe: $ 5.25; Per Serving: $ 1.31

Baked Chicken with Vegetables

Serving Size: 1/6 of recipe
Yield: 6 servings

Ingredients:

4 sliced potatoes
6 sliced carrots
1 large quartered onion
1 raw chicken - cleaned and cut into pieces, skin removed
1/2 cup water
1 teaspoon thyme
1/4 teaspoon pepper

Instructions:

1. Preheat oven to 400 degrees.

2. Place potatoes, carrots and onions in a large roasting pan.

3. Put chicken pieces on top of the vegetables.

4. Mix water, thyme and pepper. Pour over chicken and vegetables.

5. Spoon juices over chicken once or twice during cooking.

6. Bake at 400 degrees for one hour or more until browned and tender.

Per serving: 190 calories, 3.5 g fat, 26 g protein, 13 g carbohydrate, 75 mg cholesterol, 135 mg sodium

Cost: Per Recipe: $ 5.58; Per Serving: $ 0.93

Turkey Patties

Serving Size: 1 patty
Yield: 4 servings

Ingredients:

1 1/4 pound ground turkey
1 cup bread crumbs
1 egg
1/4 cup chopped green onion
1 Tablespoon prepared mustard
1/2 cup chicken broth
nonstick cooking spray

Instructions:

1. Mix ground turkey, bread crumbs, egg, onions, and mustard in a large bowl. Shape into 4 patties, about 1/2 inch thick.

2. Spray a large skillet with cooking spray. Add patties and cook, turning once to brown other side. Cook until golden brown outside and white inside, about 10 minutes. Remove.

3. Add chicken broth to skillet and boil over high heat until slightly thickened, about 1 to 2 minutes. Pour sauce over patties.

4. Serve on buns.

Per serving: 340 calories, 15 g fat, 30 g protein, 20 g carbohydrate, 165 mg cholesterol, 440 mg sodium

Cost: Per Recipe: $ 3.57; Per Serving: $ 0.89

Party-Time Pasta

Serving Size: 1 cup
Yield: 6 servings

Ingredients:

1/2 pound turkey, lean ground
1 teaspoon paprika
1 can (14 1/2 ounces) tomatoes, crushed
1 can (14 1/2 ounces) chicken broth, reduced sodium
2 cups pasta, bow-tie, uncooked
3 cups frozen vegetables such as carrots, broccoli and cauliflower, thawed

Tasty Topping:
1/2 cup chopped fresh or dried parsley
1/4 cup bread crumbs, seasoned, dry
1/4 cup grated Parmesan cheese

Instructions:

1. Heat a large nonstick pan over medium heat. Add ground turkey and paprika. Cook and stir until meat is brown and no longer pink, about 5 minutes.

2. Stir in tomatoes, chicken broth and pasta. Bring mixture to a boil. Reduce heat to medium-low. Cover and simmer until pasta is almost tender, about 10-15 minutes.

3. Remove lid. Place vegetables on top of pasta. Replace lid. Cook until vegetables are tender, about 5 minutes.

4. Prepare the Tasty Topping. Mix parsley, bread crumbs and Parmesan cheese. Sprinkle over vegetables in skillet. Cover and let sit for 3 minutes before serving.

Per serving: 210 calories, 6 g fat, 14 g protein, 26 g carbohydrate, 35 mg cholesterol, 410 mg sodium

Cost: Per Recipe: $ 6.30; Per Serving: $ 1.05

Baked Lemon Chicken

Serving Size: 2 pieces
Yield: 5 servings

Ingredients:

3 1/2 pounds chicken - skinned and cut into 10 pieces
1/4 teaspoon salt
1/4 teaspoon pepper
1 1/2 thinly sliced cloves of garlic or 1 tsp garlic powder
4 fresh thyme sprigs or 1 tsp dried thyme
3 cups thinly sliced onions
1 1/2 cups chicken stock or water
1/4 cup lemon juice
1 lemon sliced into 10 slices, seeds removed

Instructions:

1. Combine salt, pepper, garlic, and thyme.

2. Lay chicken pieces into a 11x13 baking pan. Sprinkle seasonings over chicken.

3. Combine onions, stock, and lemon juice in a sauce pan. Heat to a boil.

4. Pour hot lemon mixture around chicken. Top each chicken piece with a lemon slice.

5. Bake for 30 minutes at 400 degrees until golden brown and juices are clear.

Per serving: 450 calories, 11 g fat, 71 g protein, 16 g carbohydrate, 225 mg cholesterol, 470 mg sodium

Cost: Per Recipe: $ 4.90; Per Serving: $ 0.98

Picadillo

Serving Size: 1 cup
Yield: 6 servings

Ingredients:

1 pound turkey, ground
1 chopped onion
5 small diced carrots
2 medium zucchini or other squash
2 medium diced potatoes
1 teaspoon salt
black pepper to taste
1/2 teaspoon cumin
1 can (10 1/2 ounces) Mexican style tomato sauce
1 teaspoon cornstarch

Instructions:

1. Brown ground turkey in a non-stick frying pan.

2. Add onions, carrots, squash, potatoes, salt, pepper, and cumin. Sauté for about 5 minutes.

3. Add tomato sauce and just enough water to cover. Bring to a boil, then lower heat and simmer, uncovered, until vegetables are tender.

4. Dissolve cornstarch in about 1 Tablespoon of cold water, add to mixture, bring back to a boil until gravy thickens. Serve.

Per serving: 220 calories, 7 g fat, 16 g protein, 24 g carbohydrate, 60 mg cholesterol, 760 mg sodium

Cost: Per Recipe: $ 4.74; Per Serving: $ 0.79

Chow Mein

Serving Size: 1/6 of recipe
Yield: 6 servings

Ingredients:

6 ounces rice noodles or thin flat egg noodles
4 teaspoons oil
1 medium finely chopped onion
2 finely chopped garlic cloves
1 cup grated carrot
2 teaspoons chicken bouillon
1 teaspoon hot pepper sauce
1 cup broccoli, cut into small pieces
1 cup chopped celery
1 cup finely chopped green (or red) bell pepper
4 teaspoons soy sauce

Instructions:

1. Prepare noodles according to package directions. Drain and set aside.

2. Sauté onion and garlic with oil in frying pan for 1 minute over medium/high heat.

3. Add carrot, chicken bouillon, and pepper sauce. Stir.

4. Add broccoli, celery, and bell pepper and continue to stir.

5. Reduce heat to low and add noodles and soy sauce. Mix well over low heat for 3 to 5 minutes.

6. Add salt and pepper to taste.

Per serving: 80 calories, 3.5 g fat, 2 g protein, 12 g carbohydrate, 0 mg cholesterol, 270 mg sodium

Cost: Per Recipe: $ 2.44; Per Serving: $ 0.41

5-a-Day Bulgur Wheat

Serving Size: 1/8 of recipe
Yield: 8 servings

Ingredients:

1 medium chopped onion
1 cup chopped broccoli
1 cup shredded carrots
1 small chopped green pepper - may use red or yellow pepper
1/3 cup chopped fresh parsley or 2 Tablespoons dried
1 teaspoon canola oil
1 1/2 cups dry bulgur
2 cups chicken broth, low-sodium
8 ounces canned, drained chickpeas

Instructions:

1. Wash and chop fresh onion, broccoli, carrots, pepper and parsley (if using fresh parsley).

2. Heat canola oil in a large skillet. Add onions and cook until soft.

3. Add bulgur and stir to coat. Add 2 cups chicken broth to the skillet, bring to a boil.

4. Lower the heat, add remaining vegetables and chickpeas. Cook for 10 minutes or until the liquid is absorbed.

5. Add parsley and stir. Serve warm or cold.

Note: Bulgur comes from wheat. It is actually the kernel of wheat, cracked for cooking. It has a nutty, chewy flavor that is sure to please the healthy appetite, and contains fiber. Canola oil is a healthy choice for vegetable oil.)

Per serving: 150 calories, 1.5 g fat, 6 g protein, 31 g carbohydrate, 0 mg cholesterol, 140 mg sodium

Cost: Per Recipe: $ 3.07; Per Serving: $ 0.38

Stove-Top Casserole

Serving Size: 1/5 of recipe
Yield: 5 servings

Ingredients:

1 Tablespoon vegetable oil
1 small coarsely chopped onion
4 medium peeled and sliced (1/4 inch thick) potatoes
1 1/2 cups chicken stock
2 cups shredded green cabbage
1 cup Swiss cheese, shredded
1/4 cup chopped nuts

Instructions:

1. Heat oil in large skillet or Dutch oven. Add onions and stir over medium heat until golden.

2. Add potatoes and chicken stock. Cover tightly, reduce heat to low and simmer until potatoes are almost tender.

3. Add cabbage, cover and simmer for another 5 minutes.

4. Remove cover, sprinkle with cheese and nuts.

5. Let stand just until cheese is melted, about 2 minutes.

Per serving: 210 calories, 14 g fat, 13 g protein, 11 g carbohydrate, 20 mg cholesterol, 530 mg sodium

Cost: Per Recipe: $ 3.81; Per Serving: $ 0.76

Mexican Rice

Serving Size: 1/8 of recipe
Yield: 8 servings

Ingredients:

2 Tablespoons vegetable oil
2 cups rice, long-grain white, uncooked
3 cups chicken broth, low-sodium
1 1/2 cups finely chopped white onion
1 to 2 teaspoons minced garlic
1 can (14 1/2 ounce) Mexican or Italian style tomatoes
1/2 teaspoon salt
1 seeded and chopped green bell pepper

Instructions:

1. Heat oil in medium-size saucepan over medium heat. Sauté the rice until just golden, about 5 minutes. Add 1/2 cup of chicken broth if moisture is needed.

2. Add onions and garlic and sauté for a minute or two.

3. Stir in the tomatoes and their juice, the rest of the chicken broth, salt and bell pepper. Bring to a boil.

4. Reduce heat to low. Cover and simmer for about 20-25 minutes, or until the broth is absorbed.

Per serving: 250 calories, 4.5 g fat, 6 g protein, 46 g carbohydrate, 0 mg cholesterol, 340 mg sodium

Cost: Per Recipe: $ 3.40; Per Serving: $ 0.42

MaiN DISHeS—FISH

Baked Fish and Vegetables

Serving Size: 4 ounces fish + 1/2 cup vegetables
Yield: 4 servings

Ingredients:

4 frozen white fish fillets or cod or perch (total of 16-20 oz.)
16 ounces frozen mixed vegetables
1 small diced onion
1 teaspoon lemon juice or fresh lemon, sliced thin
1 Tablespoon parsley flakes, dried or fresh chopped
4 10x12 -inch tin foil squares

Instructions:

1. Preheat oven to 450 degrees.

2. Separate and place fish fillets in center of each tin foil square.

3. Combine frozen vegetables and diced onion in bowl and mix. Spoon vegetables around fillets.

4. Sprinkle with lemon juice (or top with lemon slice) and add parsley on top. Fold ends of tin foil together to form leak-proof seal.

5. Bake for 10 minutes. Serve.

Per serving: 350 calories, 12 g fat, 41 g protein, 17 g carbohydrate, 120 mg cholesterol, 260 mg sodium

Cost: Per Recipe: $ 5.11; Per Serving: $ 1.28

Dilled Fish Fillets

Serving Size: 1/4 of recipe
Yield: 4 servings

Ingredients:

1 pound frozen haddock or cod fillets
1 Tablespoon lemon juice
1/8 teaspoon dried dill weed
1/8 teaspoon salt
dash of black pepper

Instructions:

1. Thaw frozen fish in refrigerator overnight or thaw in microwave oven. Then, separate into 4 filets or pieces

2. Place fish in a glass-baking dish. Cover with wax paper.

3. Cook at "medium" power in the microwave for 3 minutes. Remove cover, turn fish over, and sprinkle with lemon juice and seasonings.

4. Cover and continue cooking at "medium" power for 3 minutes or until fish flakes with a fork.

Skillet method:
1. Separate into four fillets or pieces.

2. Place fish in heated fry pan. Sprinkle with lemon juice and seasonings.

3. Cover and cook over moderate heat until fish flakes when tested with a fork, about 5 minutes.

Per serving: 100 calories, 1 g fat, 21 g protein, 0 g carbohydrate, 65 mg cholesterol, 150 mg sodium

Cost: Per Recipe: $ 6.44; Per Serving: $ 1.61

Apple Tuna Sandwiches

Serving Size: 1 sandwich
Yield: 3 servings

Ingredients:

1 can (6.5 ounces) drained tuna, packed in water
1 apple
1/4 cup yogurt, low-fat vanilla
1 teaspoon mustard
1 teaspoon honey
6 slices whole wheat bread
3 lettuce leaves

Instructions:

1. Wash and peel the apple. Chop it into small pieces.

2. Drain the water from the can of tuna.

3. Put the tuna, apple, yogurt, mustard, and honey in a medium bowl. Stir well.

4. Spread 1/2 cup of the tuna mix onto each 3 slices of bread.

5. Top each sandwich with a washed lettuce leaf and a slice of bread.

Per serving: 250 calories, 3 g fat, 21 g protein, 37 g carbohydrate, 15 mg cholesterol, 360 mg sodium

Cost: Per Recipe: $ 4.02; Per Serving: $ 1.34

Tuna Quesadillas

Serving Size: 1/4 of recipe
Yield: 4 servings

Ingredients:

1 can drained tuna fish, packed in water
1 Tablespoon mayonnaise, light
4 flour tortillas
1/2 cup grated cheddar cheese, low-fat

Instructions:

1. Mix tuna with mayonnaise.

Microwave:
1. Spoon filing onto half of each tortilla. Top filling with cheese and fold tortilla in half. Microwave on high for 60 seconds. Turn the plate halfway through cooking time.

Stove:
1. Divide mixture onto two tortillas. Top with cheese and the remaining two tortillas. Spray a skillet with non-stick cooking spray. Brown quesadillas on both sides.

2. Cut in half before serving.

Per serving: 180 calories, 5 g fat, 21 g protein, 17 g carbohydrate, 15 mg cholesterol, 330 mg sodium

Cost: Per Recipe: $ 1.73; Per Serving: $ 0.43

Baked Trout

Serving Size: 1/6 of recipe
Yield: 6 servings

Ingredients:

2 pounds trout fillets or other fish, cut into six pieces,
3 Tablespoons lime juice or about 2 limes
1 medium chopped tomato
1/2 medium chopped onion
3 Tablespoons chopped cilantro
1/2 teaspoon olive oil
1/4 teaspoon black pepper
1/4 teaspoon salt
1/4 teaspoon red pepper (optional*)

Instructions:

1. Preheat oven to 350 degrees.

2. Rinse fish and pat dry. Place in baking dish.

3. In a separate dish, mix remaining ingredients together and pour over fish.

4. Bake for 15 to 20 minutes or until fork-tender.

* Used in analysis

Per serving: 310 calories, 13 g fat, 41 g protein, 4 g carbohydrate, 110 mg cholesterol, 200 mg sodium

Cost: Per Recipe: $ 9.93; Per Serving: $ 1.66

Salmon Sticks

Serving Size: 1/8 of recipe
Yield: 8 servings

Ingredients:

1 can (14.75 ounces) drained pink salmon
1/2 cup crushed saltine crackers (about 16 crackers)
1 egg
1 Tablespoon vegetable oil
nonstick cooking spray

Instructions:

1. In a large mixing bowl, combine salmon, cracker crumbs and egg.

2. Divide mixture into 8 balls and shaped into sticks about 4 inches long.

3. Lightly coat a skillet with cooking spray. Add oil and preheat the skillet on medium for 1 to 2 minutes. Add fish sticks and cook for 3 minutes.

4. Flip over and cook about 3 minutes or until golden brown.

Notes: Canned pink salmon contains soft bones that are a great source of calcium. Take out any large, hard bones, and then mash the small bones with a fork. You can do this and you will never know the bones are there once the fish is cooked. Pink salmon is "swimming" with omega-3 fatty acids—a "good" thing for your heart. So it's a good idea to get hooked on salmon.

Rinsing your hands in lemon juice and water will get rid of the fishy smell after preparing fish.

Per serving: 120 calories, 7 g fat, 11 g protein, 4 g carbohydrate, 60 mg cholesterol, 300 mg sodium

Cost: Per Recipe: $ 2.22; Per Serving: $ 0.28

Salmon Loaf

Serving Size: 1/8 of recipe
Yield: 8 servings

Ingredients:

1 can (15 1/2 ounce) salmon
2 cups breadcrumbs, soft
1 large chopped onion
1 Tablespoon melted margarine
1/4 cup diced celery
1 cup milk, 1%
1 Tablespoon lemon juice
1 teaspoon dried parsley
2 large eggs

Instructions:

1. Preheat oven to 325 degrees.

2. Drain salmon and remove skin if desired. Mash bones with meat.

3. Add the other ingredients.

4. Add enough milk so that the mixture is moist but not runny.

5. Place in a lightly oiled 9x5 inch loaf pan.

6. Bake for 45 minutes. Serve.

Per serving: 160 calories, 8 g fat, 14 g protein, 10 g carbohydrate, 90 mg cholesterol, 350 mg sodium

Cost: Per Recipe: $ 4.12; Per Serving: $ 0.52

Salmon or Tuna Patties

Serving Size: 1/9 of recipe
Yield: 9 servings

Ingredients:

1 can (15 1/2 ounce) drained salmon
1 cup whole-grain, crushed cereal or crackers
2 large eggs, lightly beaten
1/2 cup 1% milk
1/8 teaspoon black pepper
1 Tablespoon vegetable oil

Instructions:

1. Use a fork or clean fingers to flake salmon until very fine.

2. Crumble cereal or crackers into crumbs.

3. Add cereal or cracker crumbs, eggs, milk, and pepper to salmon.

4. Mix thoroughly.

5. Shape into 9 patties.

6. Heat oil in a skillet.

7. Over medium heat, carefully brown both the sides until patty is thoroughly cooked.

Note: Replace the salmon with canned tuna fish. For fun, do a combination of the two!

Per serving: 110 calories, 4.5 g fat, 12 g protein, 5 g carbohydrate, 20 mg cholesterol, 270 mg sodium

Cost: Per Recipe: $ 2.95; Per Serving: $ 0.33

Spicy Baked Fish I

Serving Size: 4 ounces
Yield: 4 servings

Ingredients:

1 pound salmon or any white fish, fresh or frozen
1/4 teaspoon paprika
1/4 teaspoons onion powder
1/4 teaspoon garlic powder
1/8 teaspoon black pepper
1/8 teaspoon dried oregano
1/8 teaspoon dried thyme
1 Tablespoon lemon juice
1 1/2 Tablespoons soft melted margarine

Instructions:

1. If using frozen fish, thaw in refrigerator according to package directions.

2. Preheat oven to 350 degrees.

3. Separate (or cut) fish into 4 pieces. Place fish in a 9x13x2 inch baking pan.

4. Combine paprika, garlic and onion powder, pepper, oregano, and thyme in a small bowl.

5. Sprinkle herb mixture (step 4 mixture) and lemon juice evenly over the fish. Then drizzle melted margarine on top.

6. Bake until fish flakes easily with a fork, about 20 to 25 minutes.

Per serving: 250 calories, 16 g fat, 23 g protein, 1 g carbohydrate, 65 mg cholesterol, 105 mg sodium

Cost: Per Recipe: $ 5.50; Per Serving: $ 1.37

Spicy Baked Fish II

Serving Size: 1 piece
Yield: 4 servings

Ingredients:

1 pound cod fillets, fresh or frozen, skinless and thawed
or other white fleshed fish
vegetable oil or spray
1/4 cup chopped onion
1/4 cup chopped green bell pepper
1 can (8 ounces) tomatoes, diced
1/4 teaspoon oregano

Instructions:

1. Preheat oven to 350 degrees. Oil or spray a baking
dish with vegetable spray.

2. Cut fish into four pieces and place in baking dish.

3. Top fish with onions, green peppers, tomatoes and
seasoning. Bake about 20 minutes or until fish flakes.

Per serving: 110 calories, 1 g fat, 21 g protein, 4 g
carbohydrate, 50 mg cholesterol, 220 mg sodium

Cost: Per Recipe: $ 6.18; Per Serving: $ 1.55

Spanish Baked Perch

Serving Size: 1/4 of recipe
Yield: 4 servings

Ingredients:

1 pound perch fillets, fresh or frozen
1 cup tomato sauce
1 small onion
1/2 teaspoon garlic powder
2 teaspoons chili powder
1 teaspoon oregano
1/8 teaspoon ground cumin

Instructions:

1. Preheat the oven to 350 degrees F.

2. Lightly grease the baking dish with butter or margarine.

3. Separate the fish into 4 fillets or pieces.

4. Put the fish pieces in the baking dish.

5. Peel the onion, and cut it into slices.

6. Stir the onion, tomato sauce and spices together in a small bowl.

7. Pour the onion-spice mix evenly over the fish pieces.

8. Bake about 10 to 20 minutes, until the fish flakes easily with a fork.

Per serving: 140 calories, 2.5 g fat, 22 g protein, 8 g carbohydrate, 50 mg cholesterol, 420 mg sodium

Cost: Per Recipe: $ 5.57; Per Serving: $ 1.39

MaiN DISHeS—veGeTariaN

Anytime Pizza, 98
Baked Lentils Casserole, 93
Broccoli Rice Casserole, 95
Butternut Squash with Black
   Beans, 89
Colorful, Hearty Skillet Meal,
   94
Colorful Quesadillas, 104
Fall Veggie Casserole, 92
Italian Bean Patties, 100
Italian Broccoli and Pasta, 90
Leafy Tofu, 97
Lentil Burgers, 102
No-Crust Spinach Pie, 88
Pasta Primavera, 84
Polenta with Pepper and
   Cheese, 87
Quiche, 86
Red Beans and Rice, 91
Scrambled Tofu, 96
Spinach and Mushroom
   Enchilada Casserole, 106
Terrific Bean Taco, 105
Tortilla Pizzas, 99
Vegetarian Chili, 85
Veggie Bean Wrap with
   Avocado and Mangos, 101

Pasta Primavera

Serving Size: 1/3 of recipe
Yield: 3 servings

Ingredients:

1 cup noodles, uncooked
1 Tablespoon vegetable oil
2 cups chopped mixed vegetables
1 cup chopped tomatoes
1 Tablespoon margarine
1/4 teaspoon garlic powder
1/8 teaspoon black pepper
3 Tablespoons Parmesan cheese

Instructions:

1. Cook noodles according to package directions.

2. While noodles are cooking, heat oil in a skillet.

3. Add vegetables and sauté until tender; stir constantly.

4. Add tomato and sauté 2 more minutes.

5. Toss vegetables with noodles and margarine.

6. Add seasonings; sprinkle with Parmesan cheese.

Per serving: 300 calories, 13 g fat, 6 g protein, 41 g carbohydrate, 20 mg cholesterol, 250 mg sodium

Cost: Per Recipe: $ 1.42; Per Serving: $ 0.47

Vegetarian Chili

Serving Size: 1/4 of recipe
Yield: 4 servings

Ingredients:

2 large onions - cut into 1/4 inch pieces
1 green bell pepper - cut into 1/4 inch pieces
3 garlic cloves
2 fresh, diced jalapeño chilies
2 Tablespoons vegetable oil
1 Tablespoon chili powder
1 Tablespoon ground cumin
1 can (28 ounce) whole tomatoes, cut into 1/4 inch
pieces (or 8 medium fresh tomatoes)
2 medium zucchini, cut into 1/4 inch pieces
2 medium summer squash, cut in to 1/4 inch pieces
1 can (16 ounce) ounces rinsed kidney beans
1 cup chopped, fresh cilantro (or coriander)
salt and pepper to taste

Instructions:

1. In a large pot sauté onions, bell pepper, garlic, and
jalapeño in oil over medium high heat for about 5
minutes, stirring often.

2. Add chili powder, cumin, half of the chopped cilantro,
salt and pepper, and continue cooking for another 3
minutes, stirring occasionally.

3. Add the tomatoes, zucchini, squash, and bring
mixture to a simmer. Simmer for 15 minutes, stirring
occasionally.

4. Add beans, and continue to simmer for another 5
minutes.

5. Serve the mixture hot. Put remaining cilantro on top.

Per serving: 330 calories, 10 g fat, 13 g protein, 49 g
carbohydrate, 0 mg cholesterol, 270 mg sodium

Cost: Per Recipe: $ 5.67; Per Serving: $ 1.42

Quiche

Serving Size: 1/6 of recipe
Yield: 6 servings

Ingredients:

1 (9-inch) baked pie shell
1 cup chopped vegetables, cooked and drained (broccoli, zucchini, or mushrooms)
1/2 cup shredded cheese
3 beaten eggs
1 cup skim milk
1/2 teaspoon salt
1/2 teaspoon pepper
1/2 teaspoon garlic powder

Instructions:

1. Preheat the oven to 375 degrees.

2. Shred the cheese with a grater. Put it in a small bowl for now.

3. Chop the vegetables until you have 1 cup of chopped vegetables.

4. Cook the vegetables until they are cooked, but still crisp.

5. Put the cooked vegetables and shredded cheese into a pie shell.

6. Mix the eggs, milk, salt, pepper, and garlic powder in a bowl.

7. Pour the egg mix over the cheese and vegetables

8. Bake for 30-40 minutes, or until a knife inserted near the center comes out clean. Let the quiche cool for 5 minutes before serving.

Per serving: 210 calories, 13 g fat, 9 g protein, 14 g carbohydrate, 115 mg cholesterol, 450 mg sodium

Cost: Per Recipe: $ 2.70; Per Serving: $ 0.45

Polenta with Pepper and Cheese

Serving Size: 1 cup
Yield: 8 servings

Ingredients:

4 cups water
1 1/2 cup corn meal, or polenta uncooked
1 can (11 ounces) whole kernel corn mixed with green
and red peppers, drained
1 can (7 ounces) green chilies
1/2 teaspoon salt
1 Tablespoon margarine or butter
6 ounce cheese, cheddar, reduced fat, shredded
1 can (15 ounces) rinsed black or pinto beans
Garnish:
cilantro sprigs
1 red bell pepper, cut into rings

Instructions:

1. In a medium sauce pan, bring the water to a boil.
Gradually add the cornmeal or polenta. Reduce heat to
low.

2. Continue stirring, add the corn, chilies and the salt.
Cook 6-8 minutes or until mixture thickens, stirring
occasionally.

3. Gently stir in the margarine, cheese and beans.

4. Remove from the heat and transfer to a serving dish.

5. Garnish with red bell pepper rings and cilantro.

Per serving: 240 calories, 5 g fat, 11 g protein, 37 g
carbohydrate, 5 mg cholesterol, 580 mg sodium

Cost: Per Recipe: $ 4.38; Per Serving: $ 0.55

No-Crust Spinach Pie

Serving Size: 1/2 to 1/3 of recipe
Yield: 2 servings

Ingredients:

2 Tablespoons butter
2 large eggs
1/2 cup flour
1/2 cup 1% milk
2 minced garlic cloves or 1/2 teaspoon garlic powder
1/2 teaspoon baking powder
4 ounces mozzarella
2 cups chopped, fresh spinach

Instructions:

1. Preheat oven to 350 degrees.

2. Melt butter or margarine in an 8 inch baking pan.

3. Beat eggs well. Add flour, milk, garlic and baking powder. Pour into baking pan. Stir in cheese and spinach.

4. Bake for 30-35 minutes or until firm and the cheese is slightly golden brown.

Per serving: 310 calories, 16 g fat, 13 g protein, 29 g carbohydrate, 165 mg cholesterol, 410 mg sodium

Cost: Per Recipe: $ 1.72; Per Serving: $ 0.86

Butternut Squash with Black Beans

Serving Size: 1 cup
Yield: 6 servings

Ingredients:

1 small butternut squash
1 teaspoon vegetable oil
1 small chopped onion
1/4 teaspoon garlic powder
1/4 cup red wine vinegar
1/4 cup water
2 cans (16 ounces each) rinsed and drained black beans
1/2 teaspoon oregano

Instructions:

1. Heat the squash in the microwave on high heat for 1-2 minutes. This will soften the skin.

2. Carefully peel the squash with a vegetable peeler or small knife.

3. Cut the squash into 1/2 inch cubes.

4. Peel and chop the onion.

5. In a large pan, heat the oil. Add the onion, garlic powder, and squash.

6. Cook for 5 minutes on medium heat.

7. Add vinegar and water. Cook on low heat till the squash is tender, about 10 minutes.

8. Add the beans and oregano. Cook until the beans are heated through.

Per serving: 120 calories, 1 g fat, 6 g protein, 28 g carbohydrate, 0 mg cholesterol, 270 mg sodium

Cost: Per Recipe: $ 3.09; Per Serving: $ 0.52

Italian Broccoli and Pasta

Serving Size: 1 1/4 cups
Yield: 4 servings

Ingredients:

2 cups fettuccini noodles, uncooked
3 Tablespoons chopped green onion (also called scallions)
2 cups broccoli florets
1/2 teaspoon dried thyme
1/2 teaspoon dried oregano
1/2 teaspoon black pepper
1 can (14.5 ounce) stewed tomatoes
2 teaspoons grated Parmesan cheese

Instructions:

1. Cook noodles according to package instructions (do not include oil or salt), and drain.

2. Spray a medium skillet with nonstick cooking spray; stir-fry onion and broccoli for 3 minutes over medium heat.

3. Add seasonings (but not the Parmesan cheese) and tomatoes; simmer until heated through.

4. Spoon vegetable mixture over noodles and top with Parmesan cheese.

Per serving: 240 calories, 1.5 g fat, 9 g protein, 48 g carbohydrate, 0 mg cholesterol, 260 mg sodium

Cost: Per Recipe: $ 3.13; Per Serving: $ 0.78

Red Beans and Rice

Serving Size: 1/8 of recipe
Yield: 8 servings

Ingredients:

1 pound red beans, dry
8 cups water
1 1/2 cups chopped onion
1 cup chopped celery
4 bay leaves
3 Tablespoons chopped garlic
3 Tablespoons chopped parsley
2 teaspoons crushed, dried thyme
1 teaspoon salt
1 teaspoon black pepper
1 cup chopped green pepper

Instructions:

1. Pick through beans to remove bad beans. Rinse beans thoroughly.

2. In a 5-quart pot, mix beans, water, onion, celery and bay leaves. Bring to boiling; reduce heat.

3. Cover and cook over low heat for about 1-1/2 hours or until beans are tender. Stir and mash beans against side of pan.

4. Add garlic, parsley, thyme, salt, black pepper, and green pepper.

5. Cook uncovered, over low heat, until creamy, about 30 minutes. Remove bay leaves. Serve over hot cooked rice.

Per serving: 210 calories, 1 g fat, 14 g protein, 39 g carbohydrate, 0 mg cholesterol, 310 mg sodium

Cost: Per Recipe: $ 2.95; Per Serving: $ 0.37

Fall Veggie Casserole

Serving Size: 1/8 of recipe
Yield: 8 servings

Ingredients:

1 medium eggplant
4 tomatoes
1 green pepper
1 onion
1 teaspoon salt
1/4 teaspoon pepper
3 Tablespoons vegetable oil
1 garlic clove
2 Tablespoons grated Parmesan cheese

Instructions:

1. Remove the skin from the eggplant. Cut the eggplant into cubes.

2. Chop the tomatoes into small pieces.

3. Cut the green pepper in half. Remove the seeds and cut it into small pieces.

4. Chop the onion into small pieces.

5. Cut the garlic into tiny pieces.

6. Cook the first 8 ingredients in a large skillet until tender.

7. Top with the Parmesan cheese and serve.

Per serving: 90 calories, 6 g fat, 2 g protein, 9 g carbohydrate, 0 mg cholesterol, 310 mg sodium

Cost: Per Recipe: $ 4.40; Per Serving: $ 0.55

Baked Lentils Casserole

Serving Size: 1/5 of recipe
Yield: 5 servings

Ingredients:

1 cup rinsed lentils
3/4 cup water
1/2 teaspoon salt
1/4 teaspoon pepper (optional)
1/2 cup chopped onion
1/4 teaspoon garlic powder (optional)
1 can (16 ounces) tomatoes
2 thinly sliced carrots
1/2 cup cheddar cheese, shredded

Instructions:

1. Combine lentils, water, seasonings, onion, and tomatoes.

2. Place in 2 quart casserole dish.

3. Cover tightly with lid or foil.

4. Bake at 350 degrees for 30 minutes.

5. Remove from oven and add carrots. Stir.

6. Cover and bake 30 minutes longer.

7. Remove cover and sprinkle cheese on top.

8. Bake, uncovered 5 minutes, until cheese melts.

Per serving: 210 calories, 3.5 g fat, 13 g protein, 32 g carbohydrate, 10 mg cholesterol, 240 mg sodium

Cost: Per Recipe: $ 3.04; Per Serving: $ 0.61

Colorful, Hearty Skillet Meal

Serving Size: 1 1/2 cup
Yield: 4 servings

Ingredients:

1 package (10 ounce) frozen mustard greens, or collard greens, spinach, or broccoli
1 can (32 ounces) stewed tomatoes, no salt added
1 cup brown rice, cooked
1 can (15 ounces) ounce white beans, rinsed and drained
pepper to taste
other spices to taste oregano, basil, or hot pepper (optional)

Instructions:

1. Steam greens in the stewed tomatoes using a small pan, pot, or electric skillet on medium-high heat.

2. Cook greens 10 to 20 minutes, until they are as soft as you like them. Stir gently.

3. Add the rice, canned beans, and seasonings.

4. Cook until heated through.

Per serving: 260 calories, 1 g fat, 13 g protein, 50 g carbohydrate, 0 mg cholesterol, 55 mg sodium

Cost: Per Recipe: $ 3.45; Per Serving: $ 0.86

Broccoli Rice Casserole

Serving Size: 1/12 of recipe
Yield: 12 servings

Ingredients:

1 1/2 cup rice
3 1/2 cups water
1 medium chopped onion
1 can (10 3/4 ounce) condensed cream of mushroom, or chicken, or celery or cheese soup
1 1/2 cups 1% milk
2 - 10 ounce packages frozen chopped broccoli or cauliflower or mixed vegetables
1/2 pound grated or sliced cheese
3 Tablespoons margarine or butter

Instructions:

1. Preheat oven to 350 degrees and grease on 12x9x2 inch baking pan.

2. In a saucepan mix rice, salt, and 3 cups of water and bring to a boil.

3. Cover and simmer for 15 minutes. Remove saucepan from heat and set aside for additional 15 minutes.

4. Sauté onions in margarine or butter until tender.

5. Mix soup, milk, 1/2 cup of water, onions, and rice. Spoon mixture into baking pan.

6. Thaw and drain the vegetables and then spread over the rice mixture.

7. Spread the cheese evenly over the top and bake at 350 degrees for 25-30 minutes until cheese is melted and rice is bubbly.

Per serving: 240 calories, 11 g fat, 9 g protein, 26 g carbohydrate, 20 mg cholesterol, 340 mg sodium

Cost: Per Recipe: $ 6.06; Per Serving: $ 0.51

Scrambled Tofu

Serving Size: 1/4 of recipe
Yield: 4 servings

Ingredients:

1 container (20 ounces) tofu
1 Tablespoon butter
2 eggs
salt and pepper to taste
(optional) bean sprouts or chop suey mix, garlic, watercress, mushrooms, cheese, bell pepper, green onions

Instructions:

1. Drain tofu.

2. In small bowl, dice or mash tofu. For optional ingredients, crush garlic and/or slice watercress, mushrooms, cheese, bell peppers, and green onions.

3. In a pan, melt butter. Add tofu. Add optional ingredients. Sauté over medium heat until lightly browned.

4. Beat eggs and add to tofu mixture. Cook until firm.

5. Sprinkle with salt and pepper to taste.

6. Stir and cook until firm.

Per serving: 140 calories, 10 g fat, 13 g protein, 1 g carbohydrate, 115 mg cholesterol, 55 mg sodium

Cost: Per Recipe: $ 2.74; Per Serving: $ 0.69

Leafy Tofu

Serving Size: 1/6 of recipe
Yield: 6 servings

Ingredients:

1 container (20 ounces) tofu
1-2 Tablespoons oil
2 bunches fresh spinach
2 Tablespoons soy sauce
1 teaspoon toasted sesame seeds

Instructions:

1. Drain tofu.

2. Dice tofu into 1-inch cubes.

3. Tear spinach into bite-sized pieces.

4. In a large pan, heat oil and sauté tofu cubes for a few minutes. Move tofu to the center of the pan.

5. Add spinach, and soy sauce. Mix.

6. Cover pan and cook until spinach is wilted.

7. Sprinkle toasted sesame seeds.

Note: May use other dark green leafy vegetables.

Per serving: 120 calories, 7 g fat, 12 g protein, 6 g carbohydrate, 0 mg cholesterol, 440 mg sodium

Cost: Per Recipe: $ 4.16; Per Serving: $ 0.69

Anytime Pizza

Serving Size: 1 slice of bread
Yield: 2 servings

Ingredients:

1/2 loaf Italian or French bread split lengthwise, or 2 split English muffins
1/2 cup pizza sauce
1/2 cup cheese, low-fat shredded mozzarella or cheddar
3 Tablespoons chopped green pepper
3 Tablespoons sliced mushrooms, fresh or canned
other vegetable toppings as desired (optional)
Italian seasoning (optional)

Instructions:

1. Toast the bread or English muffin until slightly brown.

2. Top bread or muffin with pizza sauce, vegetables and low-fat cheese.

3. Sprinkle with Italian seasonings as desired.

4. Return bread to toaster oven (or regular oven preheated to 350 degrees).

5. Heat until cheese melts.

Per serving: 180 calories, 7 g fat, 12 g protein, 21 g carbohydrate, 15 mg cholesterol, 540 mg sodium

Cost: Per Recipe: $ 1.98; Per Serving: $ 0.99

Tortilla Pizzas

Serving Size: 1 pizza
Yield: 6 servings

Ingredients:

12 small flour or corn tortillas
vegetable oil or margarine
1 can (16 ounce) refried beans
1/4 cup chopped onion
2 ounces diced fresh or canned green chili peppers
6 Tablespoons red taco sauce
3 cups chopped vegetables, such as broccoli, mushrooms, spinach, and red bell pepper
1/2 cup cheese, shredded part-skim mozzarella
1/2 cup chopped, fresh cilantro

Instructions:

1. Brush one side of each of two tortillas with water. Press the wet sides of the tortillas together to form a thick crust for the pizza.

2. Brush the outside of the tortillas with a small amount of oil or margarine. Evenly brown both sides in a heated frying pan. Repeat with the rest of the tortillas. Set aside.

3. Heat refried beans, onion, and half of the chili peppers together in a medium saucepan, stirring occasionally. Remove from heat.

4. Spread about 1/3 cup of the bean mixture on each tortilla pizza. Sprinkle with 1 Tablespoon taco sauce, then top with 1/2 cup of the chopped vegetables, 1 teaspoon chili peppers, and 1 Tablespoon cheese for each pizza.

5. Return to frying pan and heat until cheese melts. Top with cilantro, if desired. Serve immediately.

Per serving: 370 calories, 9 g fat, 15 g protein, 63 g carbohydrate, 5 mg cholesterol, 950 mg sodium

Cost: Per Recipe: $ 3.75; Per Serving: $ 0.62

Italian Bean Patties

Serving Size: 1 patty
Yield: 8 servings

Ingredients:

2 cups cooked beans
1 beaten egg
1/2 teaspoon garlic powder
1/2 teaspoon onion powder
2 teaspoons Italian Seasoning
1 cup dry bread crumbs or cracker crumbs
2 Tablespoons cornmeal or all purpose flour
2 Tablespoons vegetable oil

Instructions:

1. In a large bowl, mash beans. Add egg and spices and stir to mix evenly.

2. Stir in bread crumbs. If mixture seems too wet add more breadcrumbs, 1 Tablespoon at a time until mixture resembles meatloaf.

3. Shape into little sausages or patties. Roll in cornmeal or flour.

4. Fry slowly in vegetable oil over medium heat until crusty and golden brown.

Notes:
• Serve in place of hamburgers and add toppings
• Serve in place of breakfast sausage

Per serving: 160 calories, 5 g fat, 6 g protein, 22 g carbohydrate, 25 mg cholesterol, 340 mg sodium

Cost: Per Recipe: $ 1.19; Per Serving: $ 0.15

Veggie Bean Wrap with Avocado and Mangos

Serving Size: 1 wrap
Yield: 4 servings

Ingredients:

2 seeded and chopped green or red bell peppers
1 peeled and sliced onion
1 can (15 ounce) drained and rinsed black beans, 50% less salt
2 chopped mangos
1 lime, juiced
1/2 cup chopped fresh cilantro
1 peeled and diced avocado
4 - 10 inch flour tortillas, fat-free

Instructions:

1. In a nonstick pan, sauté bell peppers and onion for 5 minutes over medium heat. Add beans, stir well. Reduce heat to low and simmer about 5 minutes.

2. In a small bowl, combine mangos, lime juice, cilantro, and avocado. Reserve 1/2 mixture for topping.

3. Fill warmed tortillas with 1/4 bean mixture and 1/4 mango mixture.

4. Fold ends of the tortillas over. Roll up to make wraps. Top veggie bean wraps with remaining mango mixture.

Per serving: 460 calories, 13 g fat, 13 g protein, 80 g carbohydrate, 0 mg cholesterol, 690 mg sodium

Cost: Per Recipe: $ 3.58; Per Serving: $ 0.89

Lentil Burgers

Serving Size: 1 burger
Yield: 8 servings

Ingredients:

1 1/4 cups lentils
3 cups water
1 cup chopped onion
1 cup grated carrots
3 cups fresh bread crumbs
1 egg
1 teaspoon garlic powder
1/2 teaspoon crumbled leaf oregano
1/2 teaspoon salt
3 Tablespoons margarine
4 ounces sliced cheddar cheese

Instructions:

1. Place lentils in a colander, rinse in cold water and drain.

2. In a medium saucepan, bring water to a boil. Add lentils, reduce heat to low, cover and cook for 15 minutes.

3. Add onion and carrots. Cook 15 minutes more or until lentils are tender.

4. Remove from heat and cool slightly.

5. Stir in bread crumbs, egg, garlic powder, oregano and salt.

6. Melt margarine in large skillet. Drop lentil mixture by rounded 1/2 cupfuls into hot margarine. Flatten mounds into patties and cook until firm and golden brown on both sides.

7. Top each patty with a thin slice of cheese. Serve immediately.

Per serving: 390 calories, 13 g fat, 17 g protein, 52 g carbohydrate, 40 mg cholesterol, 610 mg sodium

Cost: Per Recipe: $ 3.50; Per Serving: $ 0.44

Colorful Quesadillas

Serving Size: 4 wedges or 1 quesadilla
Yield: 8 servings

Ingredients:

8 ounces cream cheese, fat-free
1/4 teaspoon garlic powder
8 small flour tortillas
1 cups chopped sweet red pepper
1 cup shredded low-fat cheese
2 cup fresh spinach leaves or 9 oz. frozen, thawed and squeezed dry

Instructions:

1. In a small bowl, mix the cream cheese and garlic powder.

2. Spread about 2 tablespoons of the cheese mixture on each tortilla.

3. Sprinkle about 2 tablespoons bell pepper and 2 tablespoons cheese on one half of each tortilla.

4. Add spinach: 1/4 cup if using fresh leaves OR 2 Tablespoons if using frozen. Fold tortillas in half.

5. Heat a large skillet over medium heat until hot. Put 2 folded tortillas in skillet and heat for 1-2 minutes on each side or until golden brown.

6. Remove quesadillas from skillet, place on platter and cover with foil to keep warm while cooking the remainder.

7. Cut each quesadilla into 4 wedges. Serve warm.

Per serving: 160 calories, 3.5 g fat, 11 g protein, 21 g carbohydrate, 5 mg cholesterol, 420 mg sodium

Cost: Per Recipe: $ 3.78; Per Serving: $ 0.47

Terrific Bean Taco

Serving Size: 1/8 of recipe
Yield: 8 servings

Ingredients:

1 small chopped onion
2 teaspoons vegetable oil
2 cups refried beans
8 taco shells or flour tortillas, wheat or white
1/4 head lettuce, chopped
2 chopped tomatoes
1 cup shredded cheese
taco sauce (optional)

Instructions:

1. Stir fry chopped onion in vegetable oil.

2. Stir in refried beans. Heat thoroughly.

3. Spread refried bean mixture in taco shell or on tortilla.

4. Sprinkle with shredded cheese, lettuce, chopped tomatoes and taco sauce, as desired.

Per serving: 190 calories, 10 g fat, 8 g protein, 21 g carbohydrate, 15 mg cholesterol, 390 mg sodium

Cost: Per Recipe: $ 5.35; Per Serving: $ 0.67

Spinach and Mushroom Enchilada Casserole

Serving Size: 1/8 of recipe
Yield: 8 servings

Ingredients:

2 teaspoons olive oil
1 medium chopped onion
2 minced garlic clove
3 seeded, de-veined and minced yellow banana chili peppers
3 pounds sliced mushrooms
1 can (14 ounce) enchilada sauce (preferably green)
8 - 6 inch corn tortillas, cut in half
1/4 teaspoon salt
1/2 teaspoon dried oregano leaves
2 packages (10 ounce) frozen chopped spinach, thawed
6 1/2 ounces grated reduced-fat Monterey Jack cheese

Instructions:

1. Heat oil in a very large non-stick skillet. Add onion, garlic and peppers and stir. Add mushrooms and cook about 15 to 20 minutes, until liquid evaporates. (If pan is not large enough, cook mushrooms in batches.)

2. Pour half of the enchilada sauce into a 13x9-inch baking dish.

3. Arrange 8 tortilla halves over the sauce in the baking dish. Preheat the oven to 350 degrees. When mushrooms are cooked, stir in the salt and crumble in the oregano leaves. Drain the spinach, squeeze it dry and mix it thoroughly with the mushroom mixture. Spoon half the mushroom mixture into the baking dish, carefully covering tortillas.

4. Set aside 1/4 cup (about 1 ounce) of grated cheese. Sprinkle the rest of the cheese on top of the mushroom mixture. Layer with the remaining 8 tortilla halves, then the remaining mushroom mixture and enchilada sauce. Sprinkle top of casserole with the remaining 1/4 cup

cheese. Cover baking dish with foil and bake for 30 minutes, or until casserole is steaming hot in the center.

Note: Allow casserole to stand at room temperature 5 minutes before serving. Serve with pinto or black beans and salad.

Per serving: 240 calories, 11 g fat, 16 g protein, 26 g carbohydrate, 25 mg cholesterol, 350 mg sodium

Cost: Per Recipe: $ 15.89; Per Serving: $ 1.99

SIDE DISHES

Old-Fashioned Stuffing

Serving Size: 1/10 of recipe
Yield: 10 servings

Ingredients:

4 Tablespoons margarine or butter
2 cups diced celery
1 cup chopped onion
8 cups bread cubes, dried from whole wheat bread
2 Tablespoons chopped fresh or dried parsley
1/4 cup sliced mushrooms
1 teaspoon ground sage
3/4 teaspoon poultry seasoning
1 teaspoon black pepper
3 cups broth, chicken or turkey

Instructions:

1. Toast bread cubes and set aside for later use.

2. Melt margarine or butter in medium size fry pan.

3. Add celery and onion; cook until tender, about 10 minutes.

4. Add parsley, mushrooms, seasoning and broth. Cook for 5 minutes.

5. Remove from heat and add the toasted bread cubes. Cover and let stand 10 minutes. Serve immediately.

Per serving: 140 calories, 6 g fat, 4 g protein, 18 g carbohydrate, 0 mg cholesterol, 270 mg sodium

Cost: Per Recipe: $ 3.65; Per Serving: $ 0.36

Glazed Carrots

Serving Size: 1/6 of recipe
Yield: 6 servings

Ingredients:

2 Tablespoons margarine
1 1/2 pounds carrots
1 cup water
1/4 teaspoon pepper
2 teaspoons sugar

Instructions:

1. Peel the carrots. Cut in half lengthwise, then cut into 1 inch pieces.

2. Melt the margarine in a heavy saucepan on low heat.

3. Add the carrots. Stir to coat them with the margarine.

4. Add the water, salt and pepper.

5. Cover and simmer for about 15 minutes until tender.

6. Drain the water.

7. Add the sugar.

8. Cover the pan.

9. Shake the pan back and forth on the burner for 1 minute.

10. Cook for 1 more minute, until the carrots are glazed but not brown.

Per serving: 80 calories, 4 g fat, 1 g protein, 12 g carbohydrate, 0 mg cholesterol, 210 mg sodium

Cost: Per Recipe: $ 1.57; Per Serving: $ 0.26

Broccoli and Corn Bake

Serving Size: 1/6 of recipe
Yield: 6 servings

Ingredients:

1 can (15 ounce) cream-style corn
1 package (10 ounce) frozen broccoli, cooked
1 beaten egg
1/2 cup crushed cracker crumbs
1/4 cup margarine
Topping:
6 crushed saltine crackers
1 Tablespoon melted margarine

Instructions:

1. Mix corn, broccoli, egg, cracker crumbs and margarine together in greased 1 1/2 quart casserole.

2. Mix topping ingredients together in small bowl. Sprinkle over corn mixture.

3. Bake at 350 degrees for 40 minutes.

Per serving: 200 calories, 11 g fat, 4 g protein, 21 g carbohydrate, 35 mg cholesterol, 430 mg sodium

Cost: Per Recipe: $ 1.82; Per Serving: $ 0.30

Cabbage Comfort

Serving Size: 1/4 of recipe
Yield: 4 servings

Ingredients:

1 sliced onion
1 teaspoon vegetable oil
1 pound sliced cabbage
1/4 teaspoon salt
1/4 teaspoon black pepper
1 teaspoon caraway seeds

Instructions:

1. Heat oil in a large sauté pan.

2. Sauté onion over medium heat, until light brown, about 5 to 6 minutes.

3. Add sliced cabbage, salt, black pepper, and caraway seeds.

4. Stir and cook for 30 minutes.

5. Serve immediately.

Per serving: 50 calories, 1.5 g fat, 2 g protein, 9 g carbohydrate, 0 mg cholesterol, 170 mg sodium

Cost: Per Recipe: $ 0.92; Per Serving: $ 0.23

Brussels Sprouts with Mushroom Sauce

Serving Size: 1/2 of recipe
Yield: 2 servings

Ingredients:

1/2 pound Brussels sprouts or broccoli, cabbage, kale, collards, or turnips
1/2 cup chicken broth, low-sodium
1 teaspoon lemon juice
1 teaspoon spicy brown mustard
1/2 teaspoon dried thyme
1/2 cup sliced mushrooms

Instructions:

1. Trim Brussels sprouts and cut in half. Steam until tender (about 6 to 10 minutes), or microwave on high for 3 to 4 minutes.

2. In a non-stick pot bring the broth to a boil.

3. Mix in the lemon juice, mustard, and thyme. Add the mushrooms.

4. Boil until the broth is reduced by half, about 5 to 8 minutes.

5. Add the Brussels sprouts (or other cooked vegetable).

6. Toss well to coat with the sauce.

Per serving: 70 calories, 1 g fat, 4 g protein, 10 g carbohydrate, 0 mg cholesterol, 85 mg sodium

Cost: Per Recipe: $ 1.44; Per Serving: $ 0.72

Spanish Cauliflower

Serving Size: 1/2 cup
Yield: 6 servings

Ingredients:

1 Tablespoon vegetable oil
1 medium onion
1/4 teaspoon garlic powder
1 large head of cauliflower
2 large tomatoes
1/2 teaspoon black pepper
1 Tablespoon dried parsley
1/4 cup grated Parmesan cheese

Instructions:

1. Chop the cauliflower into 2 inch pieces.

2. Peel the onion. Chop it into small pieces.

3. Chop the tomatoes into small pieces.

4. Put the cauliflower in a pan. Add 1 inch of water.

5. Cook over medium heat, and let it boil for 3 minutes.

6. In a large pan, heat the oil, and add the onion. Cook over medium heat for 3 to 5 minutes.

7. Add the garlic and cauliflower. Cook while stirring for 3 minutes, until lightly browned.

8. Add the tomatoes and pepper. Cook for 5 more minutes.

9. Serve with a sprinkle of parsley and cheese.

Per serving: 90 calories, 3.5 g fat, 5 g protein, 12 g carbohydrate, 5 mg cholesterol, 95 mg sodium

Cost: Per Recipe: $ 4.36; Per Serving: $ 0.73

Dutch Green Beans

Serving Size: 1/4 of recipe
Yield: 4 servings

Ingredients:

1 can (15 ounces) green beans
1/2 cup bean liquid
1/4 cup brown sugar
1 teaspoon cornstarch
1/3 cup vinegar
1 small sliced onion

Instructions:

1. Drain the beans, and save the liquid from the can in small bowl.

2. Pour 1/2 cup bean liquid into the saucepan.

3. Add the cornstarch in the bean liquid. Stir well.

4. Add the vinegar and brown sugar.

5. Put on medium heat and bring to a boil.

6. Turn the heat to low.

7. Add the green beans and onions. Heat and serve.

Per serving: 80 calories, 0 g fat, 1 g protein, 20 g carbohydrate, 0 mg cholesterol, 360 mg sodium

Cost: Per Recipe: $ 1.39; Per Serving: $ 0.35

Louisiana Green Beans

Serving Size: 1/4 of recipe
Yield: 4 servings

Ingredients:

1/4 cup chopped onion
1/4 cup chopped green pepper
1/2 cup chopped celery
2 cans (16 ounces each) drained green beans
1 can (15 ounces) tomatoes

Instructions:

1. Peel and chop the onion.

2. Chop the green pepper and celery.

3. Drain the liquid from the green beans. Rinse with water.

4. Put the green beans in a saucepan. Add enough water to cover them.

5. Cook the green beans on low heat until tender. Then drain off the water.

6. Combine all the ingredients in a skillet.

7. Cook over medium heat for 15 minutes, until the celery is tender and the food is hot.

Per serving: 50 calories, 0 g fat, 3 g protein, 12 g carbohydrate, 0 mg cholesterol, 650 mg sodium

Cost: Per Recipe: $ 2.56; Per Serving: $ 0.64

Green Beans and Mushrooms

Serving Size: 1/2 cup
Yield: 6 servings

Ingredients:

1 cup chopped onion
1 cup sliced mushrooms
1 teaspoon minced garlic
1 can (16 ounce) drained, cut green beans

Instructions:

1. Spray a skillet with non-stick cooking spray.

2. Sauté onions, mushrooms, and garlic.

3. Add green beans and heat thoroughly.

Per serving: 30 calories, 0 g fat, 2 g protein, 7 g carbohydrate, 0 mg cholesterol, 200 mg sodium

Cost: Per Recipe: $ 1.90; Per Serving: $ 0.32

Broiled Tomatoes and Cheese

Serving Size: 1/3 of recipe
Yield: 3 servings

Ingredients:

3 large firm tomatoes
8 ounces cottage cheese, low-fat
1/2 teaspoon dried basil
1/8 teaspoon black pepper
1/4 cup plain bread crumbs
vegetable oil cooking spray

Instructions:

1. Wash tomatoes and cut in half.

2. Mix cottage cheese, basil and pepper.

3. Spread cheese on tomato halves.

4. Sprinkle with bread crumbs and spray with cooking spray.

5. Spray broiler pan with cooking spray. Place prepared tomatoes on a pan and broil about 10 minutes.

Per serving: 120 calories, 1.5 g fat, 12 g protein, 16 g carbohydrate, 5 mg cholesterol, 380 mg sodium

Cost: Per Recipe: $ 3.29; Per Serving: $ 1.10

Stuffed Tomatoes

Serving Size: 1/2 tomato
Yield: 6 servings

Ingredients:

1 small onion
3 large tomatoes
1 cup unseasoned breadcrumbs
2 teaspoons dried parsley
2 teaspoons dried basil
1/2 teaspoon black pepper
1/4 teaspoon garlic powder
1 Tablespoon vegetable oil
1/4 cup water (or more as needed)

Instructions:

1. Preheat the oven to 400 degrees.

2. Peel the onion. Chop it into small pieces.

3. Cut each tomato in half. Remove the part with the stem.

4. Gently squeeze each tomato half over the sink to remove the seeds.

5. Put the breadcrumbs into medium bowl. Add the spices and oil.

6. Mix well, slowly adding water to moisten the crumbs.

7. Use a spoon to press the crumb mixture into the tomato halves.

8. Lightly oil a baking pan. Place the tomatoes on the pan, with the
cut side up.

9. Bake for 15-20 minutes, until the crumbs are browned and the tomatoes are soft.

Notes: If you don't have a box of breadcrumbs, make

your own. Toast 4 slices of bread. Crush with a rolling pin or the side of a jar to make breadcrumbs. If you don't have breadcrumbs or bread, crush 3 cups of a flaked cereal instead.

Per serving: 120 calories, 3.5 g fat, 3 g protein, 18 g carbohydrate, 0 mg cholesterol, 135 mg sodium

Cost: Per Recipe: $ 2.86; Per Serving: $ 0.48

Lemon Spinach

Serving Size: 1/4 cup
Yield: 4 servings

Ingredients:

1 bunch (1 pound) of fresh spinach
1/4 teaspoon black pepper
1 Tablespoon lemon juice

Instructions:

1. Wash the spinach. Trim off the stems.

2. Put the spinach, black pepper, and lemon juice in a pan.

3. Cook over medium heat. Let the spinach boil for about 3 minutes, until just tender.

Per serving: 25 calories, 0 g fat, 3 g protein, 5 g carbohydrate, 0 mg cholesterol, 90 mg sodium

Cost: Per Recipe: $ 1.32; Per Serving: $ 0.33

Potato Spinach Casserole

Serving Size: 2 1/2" x 4" piece
Yield: 6 servings

Ingredients:

12 ounces frozen hash browns, country style, thawed
1/2 cup finely chopped, divided, green pepper
1/2 cup finely chopped, divided, onion
1/2 teaspoon salt
1/2 teaspoon black pepper
1 can (12 ounces) evaporated milk, non-fat
3/4 cup egg whites
1/2 cup cheese, reduced-fat sharp cheddar, shredded
1/2 cup cheese, reduced fat Monterey Jack, shredded
1 packed cup washed and chopped, fresh spinach
1/2 cup chopped, fresh tomatoes

Instructions:

1. Preheat oven to 425 degrees.

2. In large bowl, combine hash browns, green pepper, 1/4 cup onion, salt, and 1/4 teaspoon pepper.

3. Spray an 8x8 inch baking dish with non-stick cooking spray. Press potato mixture into bottom.

4. Bake until lightly browned around edges, 20-25 minutes.

5. In large bowl, stir together evaporated milk, egg whites, 1/4 teaspoon pepper, cheeses, spinach, remaining 1/4 cup onion, and tomatoes.

6. Reduce oven temperature to 350 degrees.

7. Pour mixture over potato crust. Bake uncovered until center is set, 40-45 minutes.

8. Cover and let stand for 10 minutes. Cut into 6 pieces. Serve hot.

Per serving: 180 calories, 4 g fat, 15 g protein, 21 g carbohydrate, 15 mg cholesterol, 480 mg sodium

Cost: Per Recipe: $ 4.14; Per Serving: $ 0.69

Spinach Stuffed Potatoes

Serving Size: 1/6 of recipe
Yield: 6 servings

Ingredients:

6 baking potatoes
1/4 cup sour cream, light
1/4 cup tofu, silken soft
1 package (10-ounce) frozen spinach, thawed and drained
1/4 cup green onion
1/4 teaspoon pepper
1/2 cup grated cheddar, low-fat
sprinkle of Mrs. Dash garlic and herb seasoning

Instructions:

1. Thaw the spinach before you cook this recipe! After it thaws, drain any extra water from the spinach.

2. Preheat the oven to 350 degrees.

3. Wash and scrub the potatoes.

4. Bake the potatoes in for 1 hour till they're tender and you can pierce them with a fork.

5. Wash and chop the green onion until you get ¼ cup onion.

6. Put the sour cream, tofu, spinach, onion, pepper and cheese in a mixing bowl. Mix well.

7. When the potatoes are baked, let them cool. Then use a spoon to scoop out the inside of the potato. Add the inside of the potato to the sour cream mix. Stir together.

8. Stuff the potato skin shells with the mixture.

9. Sprinkle the potatoes with the garlic and herb seasoning.

10. Bake the potatoes for 20-25 minutes until they're a little brown.

Notes: You can use part-skim mozzarella cheese in place of low-fat cheddar cheese.

Per serving: 90 calories, 2 g fat, 8 g protein, 11 g carbohydrate, 5 mg cholesterol, 115 mg sodium

Cost: Per Recipe: $ 4.00; Per Serving: $ 0.67

Delicious Greens

Serving Size: 1 1/2 cup
Yield: 4 servings

Ingredients:

1/2 pound mustard or collard greens rinsed, stems
removed and coarsely shredded
2 cups shredded cabbage
1 Tablespoon olive oil
2 Tablespoons minced garlic
1 chopped onion
1 Tablespoon vinegar

Instructions:

1. Rinse greens, remove stems, and tear in small pieces.

2. In a large saucepan, boil 3 quarts of water.

3. Add mustard greens, return to a boil and cook 3
minutes. Add cabbage and cook 1 more minute. Drain in
colander.

4. Heat a large nonstick skillet over medium high heat.
Add oil and sauté garlic and onion until light brown,
about 3 minutes.

5. Add greens and vinegar and cook briefly, about 3
minutes. Serve hot.

Per serving: 90 calories, 4.5 g fat, 3 g protein, 10 g
carbohydrate, 0 mg cholesterol, 20 mg sodium

Cost: Per Recipe: $ 1.84; Per Serving: $ 0.46

Smothered Greens

Serving Size: 1 cup
Yield: 5 servings

Ingredients:

3 cups water
1/4 pound turkey breast, smoked, skinless
1 Tablespoon freshly chopped hot pepper
1/4 teaspoon cayenne pepper
1/4 teaspoon ground cloves
2 crushed garlic cloves
1/2 teaspoon thyme
1 chopped scallion stalk
1 teaspoon ground ginger
1/4 cup chopped onion
2 pounds mustard greens, or turnip, collard, kale, or mixture

Instructions:

1. Place all ingredients except greens into large sauce-pan and bring to a boil.

2. Prepare greens by washing thoroughly and removing stems.

3. Tear or slice leaves into bite-size pieces.

4. Add greens to turkey stock. Cook 20-30 minutes until tender.

Per serving: 80 calories, 0.5 g fat, 10 g protein, 11 g carbohydrate, 10 mg cholesterol, 270 mg sodium

Cost: Per Recipe: $ 6.55; Per Serving: $ 1.31

Zesty Skillet Zucchini

Serving Size: 3/4 cup
Yield: 6 servings

Ingredients:

1/2 cup tomato juice, low-sodium (low-sodium V8)
1/4 teaspoon black pepper
1 medium onion
1 medium tomato
1 cup canned mushrooms
2 medium zucchini squash
1 teaspoon basil

Instructions:

1. Peel the onion. Chop it into small pieces.

2. Chop the tomato.

3. Drain the water from the can of mushrooms.

4. Cut each zucchini into thin slices.

5. Put the tomato juice and pepper in a skillet or pan. Cook on high heat for 3 minutes.

6. Add the onion, tomato, and mushrooms.

7. Reduce the heat to medium-high. Cover and cook for 5 minutes.

8. Add the zucchini. Cover and cook for another 5 to 7 minutes.

Note: Serve this dish over rice or noodles, or eat it "as is."

Per serving: 40 calories, 0 g fat, 2 g protein, 8 g carbohydrate, 0 mg cholesterol, 130 mg sodium

Cost: Per Recipe: $ 3.87; Per Serving: $ 0.65

Zucchini Au Gratin

Serving Size: 3/4 cup
Yield: 7 servings

Ingredients:

4 cups thinly sliced zucchini
1/2 cup sliced onion
2 Tablespoons water
1 Tablespoon margarine
pepper to taste
3 Tablespoons grated Parmesan cheese

Instructions:

1. Wash and slice vegetables. Place zucchini, onion, water, margarine, and pepper in a frying pan. Cover and cook over medium heat for one minute.

2. Remove cover and cook until crisp-tender, about 10 minutes.

3. Turn with large spoon to cook evenly.

4. Sprinkle with cheese; toss lightly.

5. Serve at once.

Notes: Can be served over rice or noodles. Green pepper can be used instead of onion. Summer squash can be used instead of zucchini.

Per serving: 40 calories, 2.5 g fat, 2 g protein, 4 g carbohydrate, 0 mg cholesterol, 55 mg sodium

Cost: Per Recipe: $ 1.61; Per Serving: $ 0.23

Spicy Baked Squash

Serving Size: 1/4 of an acorn squash
Yield: 4 servings

Ingredients:

vegetable cooking spray
1 acorn squash
dash of salt
2 Tablespoons margarine
3 Tablespoons brown sugar
1 teaspoon cinnamon
1/4 teaspoon nutmeg
1/4 teaspoon ginger

Instructions:

1. Preheat the oven to 400 degrees.

2. Coat the baking sheet with vegetable cooking spray.

3. Wash the squash. Cut it in half lengthwise. Remove the seeds. Cut the squash into 1/2 inch slices.

4. Place the squash on the baking sheet. Sprinkle with salt.

5. Melt the margarine on low heat in a small saucepan.

6. Add the brown sugar, cinnamon, nutmeg, and ginger to the saucepan.

7. Spread the margarine mix on the squash.

8. Bake for 20 to 25 minutes, or until tender.

Per serving: 130 calories, 6 g fat, 1 g protein, 22 g carbohydrate, 0 mg cholesterol, 80 mg sodium

Cost: Per Recipe: $ 1.30; Per Serving: $ 0.32

Butternut Squash with Black Beans

Serving Size: 1 cup
Yield: 6 servings

Ingredients:

1 small butternut squash
1 teaspoon vegetable oil
1 small chopped onion
1/4 teaspoon garlic powder
1/4 cup red wine vinegar
1/4 cup water
2 cans (16 ounces each) rinsed and drained black beans
1/2 teaspoon oregano

Instructions:

1. Heat the squash in the microwave on high heat for 1-2 minutes. This will soften the skin.

2. Carefully peel the squash with a vegetable peeler or small knife.

3. Cut the squash into 1/2 inch cubes.

4. Peel and chop the onion.

5. In a large pan, heat the oil. Add the onion, garlic powder, and squash.

6. Cook for 5 minutes on medium heat.

7. Add vinegar and water. Cook on low heat till the squash is tender, about 10 minutes.

8. Add the beans and oregano. Cook until the beans are heated through.

Per serving: 120 calories, 1 g fat, 6 g protein, 28 g carbohydrate, 0 mg cholesterol, 270 mg sodium

Cost: Per Recipe: $ 3.09; Per Serving: $ 0.52

Italian-Style Vegetables

Serving Size: 1/2 cup
Yield: 8 servings

Ingredients:

2 small zucchini, cut into 1/2 inch pieces
1/2 pound green beans, snapped into pieces
1/2 small cabbage, sliced thin or shredded
2 cups corn kernels or combination of favorite vegetables
1 medium sliced onion
1 minced garlic clove (optional)
2 Tablespoons olive oil
1 cup chopped fresh or canned tomatoes
1/2 teaspoon dry oregano

Instructions:

1. Wash and trim vegetables. Slice zucchini into 1/2 inch pieces; snap beans into pieces; thinly slice or shred cabbage.

2. Heat oil in frying pan; cook onion over medium heat until soft. Note: If using fresh green beans, cook for 2 minutes before adding onion.

3. Add vegetables and oregano.

4. Cook over medium heat for 5 to 7 minutes or until tender. Add chopped tomatoes at the last minute of cooking. Stir occasionally.

5. Serve immediately.

Per serving: 100 calories, 4 g fat, 2 g protein, 13 g carbohydrate, 0 mg cholesterol, 180 mg sodium

Cost: Per Recipe: $ 3.46; Per Serving: $ 0.43

Oven-Roasted Vegetables

Serving Size: 1/2 cup
Yield: 6 servings

Ingredients:

2 Tablespoons vegetable oil
1 Tablespoon lemon juice
1/2 teaspoon dried herbs
1/4 teaspoon salt
1/4 teaspoon pepper
3 cups cut-up fresh vegetables (such as potatoes, broccoli, carrots, cauliflower, or red peppers)

Instructions:

1. Preheat the oven to 450 degrees.

2. In a small bowl, mix the oil, lemon juice, herbs, salt and pepper.

3. Wash, peel, and cut the fresh vegetables to get 3 cups cut-up vegetables.

4. Spread vegetable on pan.

5. Coat the vegetables with the oil mixture.

6. Bake for 20 minutes. Stir after the first 10 minutes of baking.

7. Serve the vegetables while they are still hot.

Per serving: 70 calories, 5 g fat, 1 g protein, 7 g carbohydrate, 0 mg cholesterol, 110 mg sodium

Cost: Per Recipe: $ 1.38; Per Serving: $ 0.23

Roasted Root Vegetables

Serving Size: 1/4 of recipe
Yield: 4 servings

Ingredients:

4 medium-sized root vegetables (choose a variety from potatoes, rutabagas, turnips, parsnips, beets, sweet potatoes, etc.)
2 chopped carrots
1 medium chopped onion
1/4 cup vegetable oil
3 Tablespoons Parmesan cheese
Season with your favorite spices

Instructions:

1. Preheat oven to 350 degrees.

2. Cut vegetables into large chunks.

3. Place in a medium bowl and pour oil over top. Add seasonings or Parmesan and mix well.

4. Spread an even layer on a baking sheet.

5. Bake for 1 hour or until tender. Check a few vegetables to see if they are tender.

Per serving: 250 calories, 15 g fat, 5 g protein, 26 g carbohydrate, 5 mg cholesterol, 150 mg sodium

Cost: Per Recipe: $ 1.84; Per Serving: $ 0.46

Mashed Potatoes

Serving Size: 1/2 cup
Yield: 8 servings

Ingredients:

2 pounds (6 medium) potatoes
1 cup low-fat milk
3 Tablespoons margarine or butter
1 teaspoon salt
1/2 teaspoon ground pepper

Instructions:

1. Peel the potatoes, and cut them into chunks.

2. Put the potatoes in a medium saucepan with enough water to cover them.

3. Cook the potatoes on medium heat for 15 minutes or until tender.

4. Remove the potatoes from the heat. Drain the water off the potatoes.

5. Mash the potatoes with a fork or potato masher.

6. Stir in enough milk to make the potatoes smooth and creamy.

7. Add the butter, salt and pepper.

Per serving: 80 calories, 4.5 g fat, 3 g protein, 7 g carbohydrate, 0 mg cholesterol, 350 mg sodium

Cost: Per Recipe: $ 1.83; Per Serving: $ 0.23

Potatoes Au Gratin

Serving Size: 1/8 of recipe
Yield: 8 servings

Ingredients:

6 medium (3-4 inch) russet potatoes, peeled and sliced
into 1/4 inch slices
1 cup chopped raw onions
2 Tablespoons margarine
4 Tablespoons flour
1 teaspoon salt
black pepper
1 1/2 cup mild cheddar cheese, shredded
2 cups non-fat milk

Instructions:

Quickest Method:
1. Prepare a large casserole baking pan by coating
lightly with oil or cooking oil spray.

2. Place a layer of potatoes in pan, using approximately
1/4 of potatoes.

3. Sprinkle layer with 1/4 cup chopped raw onion, 1/4 of
the cheese, 1/2 tablespoon margarine, 1 tablespoon
flour, 1/4 teaspoon salt, and sprinkling of black pepper.

4. Repeat layers, making a total of 4.

5. Meanwhile heat milk over low heat.

6. Pour warm milk over all ingredients in casserole dish.

7. Bake at 350 degrees for one hour.

Creamiest Method:
1. Prepare a large casserole baking pan by coating
lightly with oil or cooking oil spray.

2. Make a white sauce by melting margarine in a small
pan. Stir in flour. Gradually add milk, stirring constantly.

3. Cook, stirring constantly, until slightly thickened. Remove from heat. Stir in cheese until melted and smooth.

4. Add salt and pepper.

5. Place a layer of potatoes and onion in a prepared casserole pan, using approximately 1/4 of the potatoes and 1/4 cup onion.

6. Spread with 1/2 cup of the sauce prepared in steps 2 and 3.

7. Repeat layers, making a total of 4.

8. Bake at 350 degrees for one hour.

Per serving: 360 calories, 9 g fat, 13 g protein, 57 g carbohydrate, 25 mg cholesterol, 490 mg sodium

Cost: Per Recipe: $ 4.60; Per Serving: $ 0.58

Roasted Herb Potatoes

Serving Size: 1/2 cup
Yield: 6 servings

Ingredients:

vegetable cooking spray
1 pound (3 medium or 3 cups cubed) potatoes
2 teaspoons vegetable oil
1/2 teaspoon rosemary
1/2 teaspoon salt

Instructions:

1. Preheat the oven to 450 degrees.

2. Coat a baking sheet with vegetable cooking spray.

3. Wash and peel the potatoes.

4. Cut the potatoes into 1/2-inch cubes, and put them in a large bowl.

5. Put the oil, rosemary, and salt in a small bowl. Stir together.

6. Pour the oil mix over the potatoes. Stir to coat the potatoes evenly.

7. Spread the potatoes on the baking sheet.

8. Bake for 25 to 30 minutes, or until lightly browned.

Per serving: 35 calories, 1.5 g fat, 2 g protein, 4 g carbohydrate, 0 mg cholesterol, 200 mg sodium

Cost: Per Recipe: $ 0.94; Per Serving: $ 0.16

Scalloped Potatoes

Serving Size: 1 1/2 cup
Yield: 4 servings

Ingredients:

2 pounds potatoes, sliced thin
2 Tablespoons margarine
1 cup sliced onion
3 Tablespoons flour
1/4 teaspoon pepper
2 cups whole milk

Instructions:

1. Wash potatoes; peel and cut into thin slices.

2. Melt 1 Tablespoon of margarine in heavy, deep skillet. Remove skillet from heat; spread half of potato slices in skillet.

3. Cover potatoes with onions. Sprinkle half of flour and pepper over potato mixture.

4. Add remaining potato slices, flour and pepper. Cut 1 Tablespoon of margarine into small pieces and place on top of potato mixture.

5. Pour milk over potato mixture; bring to boil over high heat. Reduce heat to medium low, cover, and cook until potatoes are tender, about 15 minutes.

Per serving: 220 calories, 10 g fat, 9 g protein, 24 g carbohydrate, 10 mg cholesterol, 110 mg sodium

Cost: Per Recipe: $ 2.27; Per Serving: $ 0.57

Curried Potatoes

Serving Size: 1/2 cup
Yield: 6 servings

Ingredients:

1/4 cup margarine or butter
1 small finely chopped onion
3 cups cold, boiled, cubed potatoes
3/4 cup chicken broth
1/2 Tablespoon curry powder
1/2 Tablespoon lemon juice

Instructions:

1. Peel the onion, and chop it into small pieces.

2. Peel the potatoes, and chop them into 1 inch cubes.

3. Boil the potatoes in a medium saucepan until they are soft. Drain off the hot water.

4. Add ice cold water to cover the potatoes.

5. Melt the butter on medium heat in a frying pan or skillet.

6. Cook the onion in the butter until it turns yellow.

7. Drain the water from the potatoes, and add them to the frying pan. Stir and cook until they absorb the butter.

8. Add the broth, curry powder, and lemon juice.

9. Cook until the potatoes have absorbed the broth.

Per serving: 150 calories, 8 g fat, 3 g protein, 18 g carbohydrate, 0 mg cholesterol, 260 mg sodium

Cost: Per Recipe: $ 1.72; Per Serving: $ 0.29

Taco-Flavored Potatoes

Serving Size: 6 wedges
Yield: 5 serving

Ingredients:

4 medium rose or white new potatoes
2 Tablespoons olive oil
2 (1/2 package) Tablespoons taco seasoning
3 Tablespoons corn meal

Instructions:

1. Preheat oven to 400 degrees.

2. Wash and scrub potatoes well. Cut the potatoes in half, lengthwise and then into quarters and again into eight pieces.

3. Place potatoes in large mixing bowl, toss with the olive oil until potatoes are well coated.

4. Sprinkle the seasonings and corn meal over potatoes, toss again until coated.

5. Arrange the potatoes on a non-stick baking sheet and bake for approximately 30 minutes until potatoes are golden brown.

Per serving: 110 calories, 5 g fat, 3 g protein, 11 g carbohydrate, 0 mg cholesterol, 190 mg sodium

Cost: Per Recipe: $ 1.82; Per Serving: $ 0.36

French Fries

Serving Size: 1/8 of recipe
Yield: 8 servings

Ingredients:

4 medium potatoes, cut into strips (great with sweet potatoes!)
2 Tablespoons vegetable oil
Salt and pepper to taste

Instructions:

1. Preheat oven to 450 degrees. Lightly oil a 9 x 13 inch pan.

2. Cut potatoes and pat dry on towels.

3. Spread strips of potatoes in one layer in pan.

4. Distribute remaining oil evenly over potatoes.

5. Bake for 30 to 40 minutes until potatoes are golden brown and tender. Turn frequently.

6. Season to taste.

Per serving: 50 calories, 3.5 g fat, 2 g protein, 4 g carbohydrate, 0 mg cholesterol, 150 mg sodium

Cost: Per Recipe: $ 1.47; Per Serving: $ 0.18

Maple Sweet Potatoes

Serving Size: 1/2 of recipe
Yield: 2 servings

Ingredients:

2 large sweet potatoes
2 Tablespoons yogurt, non-fat
1 Tablespoon maple syrup
1 Tablespoon orange juice

Instructions:

1. Prick potato skins with a fork. Microwave on high for 3 to 4 minute until soft and easily pierced with a knife.

2. Scoop out the pulp into a medium bowl.

3. Mash the pulp and stir in the yogurt, maple syrup, and orange juice.

4. Transfer to a microwave safe serving bowl and microwave for 1 to 2 minutes to heat through.

Per serving: 150 calories, 0 g fat, 3 g protein, 35 g carbohydrate, 0 mg cholesterol, 80 mg sodium

Cost: Per Recipe: $ 1.18; Per Serving: $ 0.59

Baked Apples and Sweet Potatoes

Serving Size: 1/6 of recipe
Yield: 6 servings

Ingredients:

5 cooked sweet potatoes
4 apples
1/2 cup brown sugar
1/2 teaspoon salt
1/4 cup margarine
1 teaspoon nutmeg
1/4 cup hot water
2 Tablespoons honey

Instructions:

1. Boil 5 sweet potatoes in water until they are almost tender.

2. After the sweet potatoes cool, peel and slice them.

3. Peel the apples. Remove the cores, and slice the apples.

4. Preheat the oven to 400 degrees.

5. Grease the casserole dish with butter or margarine.

6. Put a layer of sweet potatoes on the bottom of the dish.

7. Add a layer of apple slices.

8. Add some sugar, salt, and tiny pieces of margarine to the apple layer.

9. Repeat steps 6, 7, and 8 to make more layers of sweet potatoes, apples, and sugar/salt.

10. On the top layer of apples, sprinkle the rest of the brown sugar and margarine pieces.

11. Sprinkle the top layer with nutmeg.

12. Mix the hot water and honey together. Pour the mix over the top layer.

13. Bake for about 30 minutes until apples are tender.

Per serving: 300 calories, 8 g fat, 2 g protein, 59 g carbohydrate, 0 mg cholesterol, 320 mg sodium

Cost: Per Recipe: $ 4.08; Per Serving: $ 0.68

Sweet Potato Casserole

Serving Size: 1/10 of recipe
Yield: 10 servings

Ingredients:

1 pound sweet potatoes (about 4 medium ones)*
3 egg whites
1/2 cup sugar
12 ounces evaporated milk, non-fat
1 Tablespoon vanilla extract
1 teaspoon cinnamon
1/2 teaspoon nutmeg
1/2 teaspoon ginger

Instructions:

1. Rinse sweet potatoes in cold running water and pierce with a fork.

2. Microwave sweet potatoes on full power until tender, about 15 minutes. Turn them half way during baking.

3. Preheat oven to 400 degrees.

4. Remove skin from sweet potatoes and mash with hand beaters or food processor. Add the rest of the ingredients and mix until smooth.

5. Pour mixture in an 8 inch square baking pan. Bake until casserole is firm in the center, about 40 minutes.

6. Remove pan from oven. Allow to stand for 5 minutes then cut into 10 squares. Serve hot.

*Note: You may want to experiment with using canned sweet potatoes.

Per serving: 110 calories, 0 g fat, 4 g protein, 24 g carbohydrate, 0 mg cholesterol, 80 mg sodium

Cost: Per Recipe: $ 2.28; Per Serving: $ 0.23

Sweet Potato Patties

Serving Size: 1 patty
Yield: 6 servings

Ingredients:

3 sweet potatoes
1 cup crushed bread crumbs
1 Tablespoon vegetable oil

Instructions:

1. Wash the sweet potatoes.

2. Bake the sweet potatoes in a microwave until they are soft.

3. Remove the peels from the sweet potatoes.

4. Put the sweet potatoes in a medium bowl. Mash them with a fork.

5. Crush the bread crumbs on a cutting board with a rolling pin or jar.

6. Put the crushed bread crumbs in a small bowl.

7. Shape sweet potato into 6 small patties.

8. Roll each patty in the crushed crumbs.

9. Heat the oil in a frying pan on medium heat.

10. Brown each patty on both sides in the oil.

Note: For variety, add some finely chopped apple.

Per serving: 150 calories, 3.5 g fat, 3 g protein, 26 g carbohydrate, 0 mg cholesterol, 170 mg sodium

Cost: Per Recipe: $ 1.40; Per Serving: $ 0.23

Macaroni and Cheese

Serving Size: 1/2 cup
Yield: 8 servings

Ingredients:

2 cups macaroni
1/2 cup chopped onions
1/2 cup evaporated milk, non-fat
1 medium beaten egg
1/4 teaspoon black pepper
1 1/4 (4 ounces) cups cheese, finely shredded sharp
cheddar, low-fat
cooking oil spray

Instructions:

1. Cook macaroni according to directions. (Do not add salt to the cooking water.) Drain and set aside.

2. Spray a casserole dish with nonstick cooking oil spray.

3. Preheat oven to 350 degrees.

4. Lightly spray saucepan with nonstick cooking oil spray.

5. Add onions to saucepan and sauté for about 3 minutes.

6. In another bowl, combine macaroni, onions, and the remaining ingredients and mix thoroughly.

7. Transfer mixture into casserole dish.

8. Bake for 25 minutes or until bubbly. Let stand for 10 minutes before serving.

Per serving: 110 calories, 2 g fat, 8 g protein, 14 g carbohydrate, 30 mg cholesterol, 135 mg sodium

Cost: Per Recipe: $ 2.31; Per Serving: $ 0.29

Brown Rice Pilaf

Serving Size: 1 cup
Yield: 4 servings

Ingredients:

1 1/2 cup brown rice
3 cups water
1/4 cup chopped almonds
1 teaspoon dried parsley
1/2 teaspoon garlic powder
1/4 teaspoon black pepper

Instructions:

1. Place all ingredients in a rice cooker and cook until the water evaporates, about 30 minutes.

2. Fluff cooked rice with a fork.

Notes: This dish goes very well with fish and chicken. Add a large green salad to complete the meal. The dish may be made on the stovetop as well but may require more water.

Per serving: 290 calories, 5 g fat, 7 g protein, 55 g carbohydrate, 0 mg cholesterol, 10 mg sodium

Cost: Per Recipe: $ 0.80; Per Serving: $ 0.20

Cuban Beans and Rice

Serving Size: 1 1/2 cup
Yield: 4 servings

Ingredients:

1 teaspoon olive oil
1 Tablespoon minced garlic
1 cup chopped onion
1 cup diced green bell pepper
3 cups black beans, cooked
2 cups chicken broth, low-sodium
1 Tablespoon vinegar
1/2 teaspoon dried oregano
black pepper to taste
3 cups brown rice, cooked

Instructions:

1. Heat the olive oil in a large nonstick skillet. Sauté the garlic, onion, and green bell pepper until golden, about 3 minutes.

2. Stir in the beans, broth, vinegar and seasoning, bring to a boil then lower to a simmer; cook covered for 5 minutes.

3. Spoon over cooked rice and serve.

Per serving: 390 calories, 4 g fat, 18 g protein, 71 g carbohydrate, 5 mg cholesterol, 80 mg sodium

Cost: Per Recipe: $ 3.10; Per Serving: $ 0.78

Honey Baked Lentils

Serving Size: 1 cup
Yield: 7 servings

Ingredients:

1 pound (2 1/3 cups) uncooked lentils
1 small bay leaf (optional)
5 cups water
1/2 cup chopped onions
1 cup water
1/2 pound ground beef
1/3 cup honey

Instructions:

1. Combine rinsed lentils, bay leaf, and 5 cups water in a large saucepan. Bring to a boil. Cover tightly and reduce heat. Simmer 30 minutes. Do not drain. After cooking, discard bay leaf.

2. Chop onion. Combine onions, and 1 cup water. Add to lentils and mix.

3. Brown ground beef (if using). Drain and discard fat. Add the meat to the lentil mixture and mix.

4. Pour honey over lentil mixture. Cover tightly and bake it for one hour at 350 degrees.

Notes: Replace 1 cup water with 2 Tablespoons sugar, 1 teaspoon sugar, 1 teaspoon oregano, and 2 cups tomato sauce. Omit the ground beef for a meatless meal that is lower in calories and fat.

Per serving: 340 calories, 4 g fat, 23 g protein, 53 g carbohydrate, 20 mg cholesterol, 30 mg sodium

Cost: Per Recipe: $ 3.11; Per Serving: $ 0.44

Vegetable Fried Rice

Serving Size: 1 cup
Yield: 4 servings

Ingredients:

2 cups white rice, cooked
2 Tablespoons vegetable oil
1/2 cup chopped celery
1/4 cup chopped onion
1 package (10 ounce) frozen vegetables
1 Tablespoon soy sauce
dash of pepper

Instructions:

1. Make 2 cups of cooked white rice. Use the package directions to make the rice.

2. Chop 1/2 cup of celery and 1/4 cup of onion.

3. Heat the oil in a skillet or large frying pan.

4. Add the celery and onion. Stir fry for 2 minutes.

5. Add the vegetables to the pan. Keep stirring the vegetables until they are tender-crisp.

6. Add the cooked rice.

7. Sprinkle with soy sauce and pepper.

8. Stir fry for 2 minutes until the rice is heated and the flavors are blended.

Per serving: 210 calories, 7 g fat, 4 g protein, 33 g carbohydrate, 0 mg cholesterol, 290 mg sodium

Cost: Per Recipe: $ 1.33; Per Serving: $ 0.33

Southwestern Pepper Cups

Serving Size: 1/2 pepper
Yield: 10 servings

Ingredients:

5 medium halved and seeded green bell peppers or use red or yellow peppers
1/3 cup chopped onion
1 1/2 chopped garlic clove
3 cups rice, cooked
1 can (10 1/2 ounce) diced and undrained tomatoes with chilies
1 can (8 1/2 ounce) drained whole kernel corn
vegetable cooking spray
1/3 cup cheese, cheddar, shredded

Instructions:

1. Preheat oven to 350 degrees.

2. Blanch peppers in boiling water 2 to 3 minutes. Drain. Set aside.

3. Cook onion and garlic in oil in medium skillet over medium high heat for 3 minutes.

4. Combine rice, tomatoes with chilies, corn and onion mixture. Mix well.

5. Spoon into pepper halves, place on baking sheet coated with cooking spray.

6. Bake at 350 degrees for 10 minutes or until hot. Sprinkle with cheese.

7. Bake again at 350 degrees for 5 to 10 minutes or until hot and cheese melts.

Per serving: 110 calories, 1.5 g fat, 3 g protein, 21 g carbohydrate, 5 mg cholesterol, 210 mg sodium

Cost: Per Recipe: $ 3.78; Per Serving: $ 0.38

SOUPS & STEWS

THE TIGHT BUDGET COOKBOOK

Broccoli Potato Soup

Serving Size: 1/4 of recipe
Yield: 4 servings

Ingredients:

4 cups chopped broccoli
1 small chopped onion
4 cups chicken or vegetable broth, low-sodium
1 cup evaporated milk, nonfat
1 cup mashed potatoes, instant prepared in water
salt and pepper to taste
1/4 cup cheese, shredded cheddar or American

Instructions:

1. Combine broccoli, onion, and broth in large sauce pan. Bring to a boil.

2. Reduce heat. Cover and simmer about 10 minutes or until vegetables are tender.

3. Add milk to soup. Slowly stir in potatoes.

4. Cook, stirring constantly, until bubbly and thickened.

5. Season with salt and pepper; stir in a little more milk or water if soup starts to become too thick.

6. Ladle into serving bowls. Sprinkle about 1 Tablespoon cheese over each serving.

Per serving: 200 calories, 6 g fat, 15 g protein, 25 g carbohydrate, 10 mg cholesterol, 350 mg sodium

Cost: Per Recipe: $ 3.95; Per Serving: $ 0.99

Cream of Broccoli Soup

Serving Size: 1 cup
Yield: 4 servings

Ingredients:

1 1/2 cups chicken broth
1/2 cup chopped onion
2 cups cut broccoli
1/2 teaspoon dried, crushed thyme
2 small bay leaves
2 Tablespoons margarine
2 Tablespoons flour
1/4 teaspoon salt
few dashes of pepper
1 cup nonfat milk
dash of garlic powder

Instructions:

1. In a saucepan combine chicken broth, chopped onion, broccoli, thyme, bay leaf and garlic powder. Bring mixture to boiling. Reduce heat; cover and simmer for 10 minutes or until vegetables are tender. Remove bay leaf.

2. Place half of the mixture in a blender or food processor, cover and blend 30 to 60 seconds or until smooth. Pour into a bowl; repeat with remaining vegetable mixture, set all aside.

3. In the same saucepan melt the margarine. Stir in flour, salt, and pepper. Add the milk all at once, stirring rapidly with a wire whisk. Cook and stir until mixture is thickened and bubbly. Stir in the blended broccoli mixture. Cook and stir until soup is heated through. Season to taste with additional salt and pepper.

Per serving: 110 calories, 6 g fat, 5 g protein, 11 g carbohydrate, 0 mg cholesterol, 380 mg sodium

Cost: Per Recipe: $ 2.27; Per Serving: $ 0.57

Chicken Rice Soup

Serving Size: 2 cups
Yield: 8 servings

Ingredients:

6 cups broth
1 cup cooked chicken
1 cup uncooked rice
1 3/4 cup fresh chopped vegetables (such as potatoes, carrots, celery, or cabbage)
1/2 teaspoon garlic powder
1/4 teaspoon pepper
1/4 teaspoon salt
1 Tablespoon dried parsley

Instructions:

1. Use leftover cooked chicken, or cook enough chicken to make 1 cup of chicken pieces.

2. Place the cooked chicken in a large saucepan.

3. Add the broth and uncooked rice. Cover the pan.

4. Bring the broth and rice to a boil.

5. Cover the pan, and turn the heat to low.

6. Stir and simmer for 15 minutes.

7. Add the chopped onions, chopped vegetables, and seasonings.

8. Simmer for 10 to 15 minutes until the vegetables are tender.

Per serving: 160 calories, 2.5 g fat, 11 g protein, 24 g carbohydrate, 15 mg cholesterol, 150 mg sodium

Cost: Per Recipe: $ 4.94; Per Serving: $ 0.62

Chicken Pozole Soup

Serving Size: 1/6 of recipe
Yield: 6 servings

Ingredients:

1 whole chicken, skinned and cut into pieces
8 cups water
1/2 cup chopped onion
1/4 teaspoon pepper
1/4 cup chili powder
8 ounces canned tomato sauce
1/2 teaspoon dried oregano
2 cans (15 ounce) rinsed and drained hominy, white or yellow
3 cups shredded iceberg lettuce
6 lime wedges

Instructions:

1. Put chicken pieces in a large pot and cover with the 8 cups of water. Simmer over medium heat for 1 hour.

2. Add the chopped onion, pepper, chili powder, tomato sauce, and oregano to simmering chicken.

3. After the chicken is thoroughly cooked take the pieces out of the pot and remove most of the bones from the chicken and the pot.

4. Return chicken to the pot.

5. Add the rinsed hominy to the pot of chicken and simmer for another 45 minutes.

6. Serve with lettuce and a wedge of lime.

Note: To make soup even healthier, use tomato sauce with no added salt.

Per serving: 270 calories, 6 g fat, 27 g protein, 29 g carbohydrate, 75 mg cholesterol, 640 mg sodium

Cost: Per Recipe: $ 6.82; Per Serving: $ 1.14

Chicken Vegetable Soup with Kale

Serving Size: 1/3 of recipe
Yield: 3 servings

Ingredients:

2 teaspoons vegetable oil
1/2 cup chopped onion
1/2 cup chopped carrot
1 teaspoon ground thyme
2 minced garlic cloves
2 cups water or chicken broth
3/4 cup diced tomatoes
1 cup chicken, cooked, skinned and cubed
1/2 cup brown or white rice, cooked
1 cup chopped kale (about one large leaf)

Instructions:

1. Heat oil in a medium sauce pan. Add onion and carrot. Sauté until vegetables are tender, about 5-8 minutes.

2. Add thyme and garlic. Sauté for one more minute.

3. Add water or broth, tomatoes, cooked rice, chicken and kale.

4. Simmer for 5-10 minutes. Serve.

Per serving: 180 calories, 5 g fat, 17 g protein, 17 g carbohydrate, 40 mg cholesterol, 80 mg sodium

Cost: Per Recipe: $ 2.85; Per Serving: $ 0.95

Mushroom Barley Soup

Serving Size: 1 1/2 cups
Yield: 4 servings

Ingredients:

1 Tablespoon oil
1 chopped onion
2 sliced thin celery stalks
2 peeled and sliced thin carrots
2 cups sliced mushrooms
1/2 cup barley, quick cooking
1 teaspoon garlic powder
1/2 teaspoon ground thyme
3 cups chicken broth
2 cups water
1 Tablespoon chopped fresh parsley

Instructions:

1. Heat oil in large soup pot over high heat. Sauté onion, celery, carrots and mushrooms until golden, about 4 minutes.

2. Add the rest of the ingredients except for the parsley and bring to a boil.

3. Lower heat to a simmer and cook until the barley is tender, about 20 minutes.

4. Sprinkle parsley on top of soup and serve hot.

Per serving: 170 calories, 5 g fat, 8 g protein, 26 g carbohydrate, 0 mg cholesterol, 100 mg sodium

Cost: Per Recipe: $ 3.32; Per Serving: $ 0.83

Garden Barley Soup

Serving Size: 1/6 of recipe
Yield: 6 servings

Ingredients:

1 can (46 ounce) tomato juice
1 can (10 1/2 ounce) beef broth
1/3 cup regular barley
1/4 cup sugar
1 Tablespoon Worcestershire sauce
1 bay leaf
1/2 teaspoon crushed thyme leaves
1/4 teaspoon salt
2 cups coarsely chopped zucchini
1 medium chopped tomato
1/2 cup chopped green pepper

Instructions:

1. In a Dutch oven or stock pot, combine tomato juice, beef broth, barley, sugar and seasonings. Bring to boil; reduce heat.

2. Cover; simmer 1 hour.

3. Add vegetables. Return to boil; reduce heat.

4. Cover; simmer 15-20 minutes or until vegetables and barley are tender.

Per serving: 130 calories, 0.5 g fat, 4 g protein, 29 g carbohydrate, 0 mg cholesterol, 330 mg sodium

Cost: Per Recipe: $ 3.97; Per Serving: $ 0.66

Golden Split Pea Soup

Serving Size: 1 cup
Yield: 8 servings

Ingredients:

2 teaspoons vegetable oil
2 cups chopped onion
2 cups diced potatoes with skin on
1 1/2 cups yellow split peas
5 1/2 cups chicken broth, low-sodium
1 cup water
1/2 teaspoon onion powder
1 teaspoon poultry seasoning

Instructions:

1. Place the vegetable oil in a large soup pot or Dutch-oven style pan. Heat over medium-high.

2. Add the onion and sauté until golden, about 2-3 minutes.

3. Add the rest of the ingredients and mix well. Bring to a boil and then lower the heat to a simmer. Cook uncovered until the peas are tender, about 45 minutes. Serve hot.

Per serving: 240 calories, 2 g fat, 16 g protein, 41 g carbohydrate, 0 mg cholesterol, 55 mg sodium

Cost: Per Recipe: $ 3.46; Per Serving: $ 0.43

Tortellini Soup

Serving Size: 1 1/2 cups
Yield: 6 servings

Ingredients:

1 cup dried beans, Great Northern
1/4 cup brown lentils
1/4 cup green split peas
2 Tablespoons dried parsley flakes
1 Tablespoon chicken broth granules
2 Tablespoons chopped sun-dried tomatoes
2 teaspoons grated Parmesan cheese
1 teaspoon onion powder
1/2 teaspoon instant minced garlic
1/2 teaspoon thyme
3/4 cup dried tortellini
1 cup coarsely chopped carrots (optional)
1 cup coarsely chopped celery (optional)

Instructions:

1. Rinse beans. Put into a 4-5 quart heavy pot with 8 cups of water. Bring to a boil, reduce heat to medium, cover and simmer until the beans are tender (1 1/4 to 1 1/2 hours).

2. Add 4 cups water, seasonings, tortellini and, if desired, 1 cup each coarsely chopped carrots and celery. Return to boil. Reduce heat to low, cover and simmer 1/2 hour, until tortellini and vegetables are tender.

Per serving: 210 calories, 2 g fat, 13 g protein, 37 g carbohydrate, 5 mg cholesterol, 270 mg sodium

Cost: Per Recipe: $ 2.49; Per Serving: $ 0.42
Cost analysis was done using optional carrots and celery.

Italian Bean Soup

Serving Size: 1/18 of recipe
Yield: 18 servings

Ingredients:

1 can (15 ounce) great northern beans
1 can (15 ounce) red kidney beans
2 cans (15 ounce) pinto beans
1 can (46 ounce) tomato juice or V-8 juice
1 can (15 ounce) Italian style or stewed tomatoes
1 can (15 ounce) vegetable-broth, low-sodium
1 can (15 ounce) drained green beans
1 1/2 Tablespoons Italian seasoning
1 medium chopped onion
1/4 teaspoon black pepper
2 fresh garlic cloves

Instructions:

1. In a large pot, combine all ingredients.

2. Cover and simmer for 30 minutes.

3. Serve with Italian or French bread or whole-wheat rolls.

Note: Beans are a healthy high-fiber alternative to meat. Freeze leftovers in plastic sealed containers with 1/2-inch air space under the lid.

Per serving: 110 calories, 0.5 g fat, 7 g protein, 20 g carbohydrate, 0 mg cholesterol, 440 mg sodium

Cost: Per Recipe: $ 6.49; Per Serving: $ 0.36

Slow Cooker Lentil Soup

Serving Size: 1/6 of recipe
Yield: 6 servings

Ingredients:

6 cups water
1/4 cup chopped fresh parsley or 2 Tablespoons dried parsley (optional)
2 teaspoons beef bouillon or 2 cubes beef bouillon
1 1/2 cups dry lentils
2 medium sliced carrots
1 medium chopped onion
2 sliced celery stalks

Instructions:

1. Mix all ingredients together in slow cooker.

2. Cook on LOW for 8 to 10 hours or HIGH for 4 to 5 hours.

3. Serve hot with crackers or bread.

Per serving: 190 calories, 0.5 g fat, 13 g protein, 34 g carbohydrate, 0 mg cholesterol, 45 mg sodium

Cost: Per Recipe: $ 1.41; Per Serving: $ 0.24

Minestrone Soup

Serving Size: 1 cup
Yield: 6 servings

Ingredients:

16 ounces frozen vegetables, any type
30 ounces stewed tomatoes, canned, low-sodium
28 ounces broth, any flavor, canned, low-sodium
15 ounces beans, canned, any type
1 cup pasta, dry, any type

1. In a large pot, combine frozen vegetables, tomatoes, broth and beans.

2. Bring the soup to a boil and add the pasta. Then reduce to low heat. Let simmer for 6-8 minutes or until the pasta and vegetables are tender.

Per serving: 210 calories, 1.5 g fat, 11 g protein, 41 g carbohydrate, 0 mg cholesterol, 560 mg sodium

Cost: Per Recipe: $ 5.20; Per Serving: $ 0.87

Potato Soup

Serving Size: 1 cup
Yield: 6 servings

Ingredients:

1/2 cup chopped onion
1/2 cup chopped celery
6 diced potatoes
2 Tablespoons margarine
1/2 teaspoon salt
1/8 teaspoon pepper
1 cup nonfat dry milk
3 cups water
2 Tablespoons flour

Instructions:

1. Peel and chop the onion. Chop the celery. Peel the potatoes, and cut them into small cubes.

2. Melt the margarine in a large saucepan on low heat.

3. Add the onion and celery. Cook for a few minutes.

4. Add the potatoes, salt, pepper and 1 1/2 cups water.

5. Cook for 15 minutes until the potatoes are tender.

6. In a small bowl, stir together the dry milk and flour.

7. Add 1 1/2 cups water slowly, stirring as you add it.

8. Add the milk mix to the potatoes.

9. Cook until the soup is heated and slightly thickened.

10. Adjust the seasonings.

Per serving: 130 calories, 4 g fat, 7 g protein, 17 g carbohydrate, 0 mg cholesterol, 310 mg sodium

Cost: Per Recipe: $ 1.69; Per Serving: $ 0.28

Pumpkin and Bean Soup

Serving Size: 1 cup
Yield: 6 servings

Ingredients:

1 can white beans
1 small finely chopped onion
1 cup water
1 can (15 ounce) pumpkin
1 1/2 cups apple juice
1/2 teaspoon cinnamon
1/8 teaspoon nutmeg, allspice, or ginger
1/2 teaspoon black pepper
1/4 teaspoon salt

Instructions:

1. Blend white beans, onion, and water with a potato masher or blender till smooth.

2. In a large pot, add the pumpkin, juice, cinnamon, nutmeg, black pepper, and salt. Stir.

3. Add the blended bean mix to the pot.

4. Cook over low heat for 15-20 minutes, until warmed through.

Per serving: 140 calories, 0.5 g fat, 7 g protein, 30 g carbohydrate, 0 mg cholesterol, 105 mg sodium

Cost: Per Recipe: $ 1.98; Per Serving: $ 0.33

Squash Soup

Serving Size: 1/6 of recipe
Yield: 6 servings

Ingredients:

1 Tablespoon olive oil
2 medium chopped onions
2 medium chopped carrots
2 minced garlic cloves
1 cup canned tomato puree
5 cups chicken or vegetable broth, low-sodium
4 cups winter squash, cooked
1 1/2 Tablespoon dried oregano
1 1/2 Tablespoon dried basil

Instructions:

1. In a large saucepan, warm oil over medium heat.

2. Stir in onions, carrot and garlic.

3. Cook for about 5 minutes, covered.

4. Stir in the tomato puree, chicken broth, cooked squash, and herbs.

5. Bring soup to a simmer and cook, covered, for 30 minutes.

Per serving: 150 calories, 3 g fat, 7 g protein, 28 g carbohydrate, 5 mg cholesterol, 150 mg sodium

Cost: Per Recipe: $ 5.67; Per Serving: $ 0.94

Tomato Basil Soup

Serving Size: 1 cup
Yield: 4 servings

Ingredients:

1 medium chopped onion
1 Tablespoon olive oil
2 crushed garlic cloves (or 1/4 teaspoon garlic powder)
1 can (15 1/2 ounce) drained and chopped tomatoes
1 pinch ground red pepper
1 teaspoon dried basil
2/3 cup nonfat dry milk (NDM) + 2 cups water (or substitute 2 cups nonfat milk for the reconstituted NDM)
salt and pepper to taste

Instructions:

1. In a medium saucepan, cook onion in oil over medium heat, stirring frequently until golden brown, about 4 minutes.

2. Add garlic and cook 1 minute longer. Add chopped tomatoes.

3. Cook uncovered over medium heat for 10 minutes.

4. Spoon 3/4 of mixture into food processor or blender container; puree until smooth. Return to saucepan.

5. Add red pepper, basil, and reconstituted NDM to the soup. Heat until hot but do not boil. Season to taste with salt and pepper. Serve immediately.

Per serving: 120 calories, 4 g fat, 6 g protein, 18 g carbohydrate, 0 mg cholesterol, 210 mg sodium

Cost: Per Recipe: $ 1.18; Per Serving: $ 0.29

Tofu, Tomato and Spinach Soup

Serving Size: 1/4 of recipe
Yield: 4 servings

Ingredients:

1 teaspoon vegetable oil
1/2 cup chopped onion
1 minced garlic clove
6 cups water or chicken broth or 4 teaspoons or cubes
chicken bouillon
1 package (10. 5 ounce) tofu, silken, firm or extra firm,
patted dry and cut into 1/2 inch cubes
2 chopped tomatoes
3 chopped green onions (optional)
4 cups fresh spinach leaves, washed and dried, torn or
cut (if large) or one 10-ounce box frozen chopped
spinach, thawed and squeezed dry
1 Tablespoon soy sauce
1/4 teaspoon pepper
1/4 cup cilantro leaves (optional)

Instructions:

1. Heat a 3-quart saucepan over medium heat; add oil
and chopped onion. Cook onion until softened, but not
brown. Stir in garlic and cook just until fragrant.

2. Add chicken broth. Bring to a boil. Add tomatoes and
tofu. Lower heat and simmer until tomatoes are soft but
not mushy (this takes just a couple of minutes).

3. Stir in green onions, spinach, ground pepper and
cilantro. Cook just until spinach is wilted.

4. Remove from heat. Taste for seasoning. Serve hot.

Per serving: 110 calories, 5 g fat, 8 g protein, 10 g
carbohydrate, 0 mg cholesterol, 290 mg sodium

Cost: Per Recipe: $ 2.87; Per Serving: $ 0.72

Gazpacho Soup

Serving Size: 1/4 of recipe
Yield: 4 servings

Ingredients:

2 cucumbers, diced into 1/4 inch pieces
3 red bell peppers, seeded and diced into 1/4 inch pieces
3 green peppers, seeded and diced into 1/4 inch pieces
4 celery stalks, diced into 1/4 inch pieces
2 tomatoes, diced into 1/4 inch pieces
1 medium onion, diced into 1/4 inch pieces
2 lemons
2 cups tomato juice, low-sodium
3 fresh minced garlic cloves
1 Tablespoon ground cumin
1 cup fresh chopped cilantro
salt and pepper to taste

Instructions:

1. Combine all ingredients except salt, pepper and lemons in a bowl.

2. Remove 2 cups of the mixture and reserve.

3. Using a blender or food processor, puree the remaining mixture in the bowl.

4. Add 2 cups of reserved mixture to the pureed mixture.

5. Season with salt, pepper and the juice from the lemons.

6. Cover mixture and refrigerate for at lest 2 hours before serving. Serve cold, garnished with chopped cilantro.

Per serving: 140 calories, 1.5 g fat, 5 g protein, 30 g carbohydrate, 0 mg cholesterol, 65 mg sodium

Cost: Per Recipe: $ 6.45; Per Serving: $ 1.61

Corn Chowder

Serving Size: 1 1/2 cups
Yield: 4 servings

Ingredients:

1 teaspoon oil
1/2 chopped onion
1 teaspoon minced garlic
4 Tablespoons all purpose flour
3 cups nonfat milk
2 teaspoons mustard
1/4 teaspoon dried thyme
black pepper to taste
2 cups frozen corn kernels
4 Tablespoons cheddar cheese, shredded reduced-fat

Instructions:

1. Heat a large nonstick skillet over medium-high. Add the oil and sauté the onion and garlic until golden, about 2 minutes.

2. Meanwhile, place the flour, milk, mustard and seasonings in a small bowl and mix well.

3. Add the milk mixture to the skillet followed by the corn; mix well until the mixture comes to a boil and thickens, about 3 minutes. Stir frequently to keep the mixture from burning.

4. Divide into four bowls and top each with 1 Table-spoon of shredded cheese.

Per serving: 210 calories, 3 g fat, 12 g protein, 37 g carbohydrate, 5 mg cholesterol, 170 mg sodium

Cost: Per Recipe: $ 1.98; Per Serving: $ 0.50

Brunswick Stew

Serving Size: 1 cup
Yield: 8 servings

Ingredients:

1 Tablespoon vegetable oil
1 medium chopped onion
2 cups chicken broth, low-sodium
2 cups cooked, diced and boned chicken or turkey
2 cups tomatoes, canned or cooked
2 cups lima beans, canned or cooked
2 cups whole kernel corn, canned or cooked

Instructions:

1. Heat oil in a large pan. Add onion and cook in oil until tender.

2. Add all remaining ingredients. Bring to a simmer for 30 minutes at medium-low.

3. Serve.

Per serving: 200 calories, 5 g fat, 16 g protein, 22 g carbohydrate, 30 mg cholesterol, 470 mg sodium

Cost: Per Recipe: $ 5.73; Per Serving: $ 0.72

Slow Cooker Beef Stew

Serving Size: 1/6 of recipe
Yield: 6 servings

Ingredients:

1 1/2 - 2 pounds stew meat, cut into 1 inch cubes
1/4 cup all purpose flour
Salt and pepper to taste
2 cups water
2 teaspoons or 2 cubes beef bouillon
1 finely chopped garlic clove
3 sliced carrots
3 diced potatoes
1 - 2 chopped onions
1 sliced celery stalk
Add herbs as desired: bay leaf, basil, oregano, etc.

Instructions:

1. Place meat in slow cooker.

2. Mix flour, salt, and pepper in a medium bowl, and pour over meat; stir to coat.

3. Add remaining ingredients and stir to mix.

4. Cover and cook on LOW for 8 to 10 hours or HIGH for 4 to 6 hours.

5. Stir stew thoroughly before serving. If using bay leaf, discard before serving.

Per serving: 280 calories, 15 g fat, 22 g protein, 13 g carbohydrate, 70 mg cholesterol, 290 mg sodium

Cost: Per Recipe: $ 7.20; Per Serving: $ 1.20

salaDs

5-a-Day Salad

Serving Size: 1/4 of recipe
Yield: 4 servings

Ingredients:

4 cups fresh spinach
4 cups Romaine lettuce
2 cups chopped green pepper (or use red, yellow, or orange)
2 cups cherry tomatoes
1 cup chopped broccoli
1 cup chopped cauliflower
1 cup sliced yellow squash
2 cups sliced cucumber
2 cups chopped carrots
1 cup sliced zucchini

Instructions:

1. Wash all of the vegetables and mix them together in a large mixing bowl. Top this colorful meal with the nonfat or low-fat dressing of your choice.

Note: The dressing is not included in the nutritional analysis.

Each serving = 5 cups of vegetables (Eight 5-a-Day servings).

Per serving: 100 calories, 1 g fat, 5 g protein, 22 g carbohydrate, 0 mg cholesterol, 90 mg sodium

Cost: Per Recipe: $ 5.49; Per Serving: $ 1.37

Broccoli Salad

Serving Size: 1/8 of recipe
Yield: 8 servings

Ingredients:

6 cups chopped broccoli
1 cup raisins
1 medium peeled and diced red onion
2 Tablespoons sugar
8 cooked and crumbled bacon slices (optional)
2 Tablespoons lemon juice
3/4 cup mayonnaise, low-fat

Instructions:

1. Combine all ingredients in a medium bowl.

2. Mix well.

3. Chill for 1 to 2 hours.

4. Serve.

Per serving: 170 calories, 7 g fat, 2 g protein, 26 g carbohydrate, 10 mg cholesterol, 170 mg sodium

Cost: Per Recipe: $ 2.99; Per Serving: $ 0.37

Carrot Raisin Salad

Serving Size: 1/4 of recipe
Yield: 4 servings

Ingredients:

4 medium peeled and grated carrots
1/4 cup raisins
2 teaspoons sugar
juice of one lemon

Instructions:

1. In a medium bowl, thoroughly mix carrots, raisins, sugar and lemon juice.

2. Serve chilled.

Per serving: 70 calories, 0 g fat, 1 g protein, 17 g carbohydrate, 0 mg cholesterol, 45 mg sodium

Cost: Per Recipe: $ 0.86; Per Serving: $ 0.22

Corn Salad

Serving Size: 1/6 of recipe
Yield: 6 servings

Ingredients:

2 cups fresh or frozen whole kernel corn, cooked and drained
3/4 cup chopped tomato
1/2 cup chopped green pepper
1/2 cup chopped celery
1/4 cup chopped onion
1/4 cup ranch dressing, fat-free

Instructions:

1. In bowl, combine vegetables.

2. Stir in dressing.

3. Cover and refrigerate until ready to serve.

Per serving: 80 calories, 0.5 g fat, 2 g protein, 19 g carbohydrate, 0 mg cholesterol, 130 mg sodium

Cost: Per Recipe: $ 2.02; Per Serving: $ 0.34

Cucumber Salad

Serving Size: 1 cup
Yield: 2 servings

Ingredients:

1 large peeled and thinly sliced cucumber
2 Tablespoons yogurt, low-fat
1 Tablespoon vinegar
1 Tablespoon vegetable oil
1 Tablespoon water
1 teaspoon dill weed (optional)
dash of pepper

Instructions:

1. Peel and thinly slice cucumber.

2. Mix all other ingredients in the mixing bowl.

3. Add cucumber slices and stir until coated.

4. Chill until serving.

Per serving: 90 calories, 7 g fat, 2 g protein, 4 g carbohydrate, 0 mg cholesterol, 15 mg sodium

Cost: Per Recipe: $ 0.81; Per Serving: $ 0.41

Cucumber Salad with Tomatoes and Couscous

Serving Size: 1/4 of recipe
Yield: 4 servings

Ingredients:

2 cups diced cucumber
1 cup seeded and diced tomato
1/4 cup chopped sweet onion
2 cup couscous or rice, cooked
2 teaspoons chopped dried or fresh dill weed
1/2 cup Italian salad dressing, low-fat

Instructions:

1. Toss together the cucumbers, tomatoes, onions, couscous (or rice), dill, and salad dressing.

2. Chill for 1 hour before serving.

Per serving: 150 calories, 3.5 g fat, 4 g protein, 25 g carbohydrate, 0 mg cholesterol, 280 mg sodium

Cost: Per Recipe: $ 1.89; Per Serving: $ 0.47

Coleslaw

Serving Size: 3/4 cup
Yield: 4 servings

Ingredients:

2 cups shredded cabbage
1/4 cup cider vinegar
1/4 cup water
2 Tablespoons sugar
1/2 teaspoon mustard
1/4 teaspoon black pepper

Instructions:

1. Wash and shred the cabbage with a knife or grater. Put in a mixing bowl.

2. Bring the vinegar and water to a boil in the saucepan. Remove from heat and add other ingredients except cabbage to the saucepan.

3. Continue to cook this mixture in the saucepan until the sugar is dissolved and hot, then pour over the shredded cabbage.

4. Toss. Refrigerate until chilled to blend flavors.

Note: Refrigeration is needed before serving.

Per serving: 40 calories, 0 g fat, 1 g protein, 9 g carbohydrate, 0 mg cholesterol, 5 mg sodium

Cost: Per Recipe: $ 0.36; Per Serving: $ 0.09

Garden Orchard Salad

Serving Size: 1/4 of recipe
Yield: 4 servings

Ingredients:

1 1/2 cups coarsely chopped broccoli florets
1/2 cup grated carrots
1/2 cup coarsely chopped cauliflower
1/2 cup chopped, cored and diced, not peeled, apple
1/4 cup sliced green onion
1/2 cup yogurt, nonfat vanilla
1/4 cup chopped peanuts, unsalted, dry-roasted

Instructions:

1. Mix all ingredients together in serving bowl.

2. Cover and refrigerate for 2 hours or longer to allow flavors to blend. Serve cold.

Per serving: 110 calories, 5 g fat, 5 g protein, 14 g carbohydrate, 0 mg cholesterol, 45 mg sodium

Cost: Per Recipe: $ 1.66; Per Serving: $ 0.41

Simple Mexican Salad

Serving Size: 1/4 of recipe
Yield: 4 servings

Ingredients:

2 cucumbers
2 oranges
1 lemon or lime (the juice)
1/2 teaspoon chili powder
1/2 teaspoon salt

Instructions:

1. Wash the cucumbers, oranges and lemon or lime under cold running water.

2. Slice the cucumbers. Peel and cut the oranges into small pieces.

3. Place cucumber and oranges in a medium size bowl. Add chili powder, lemon or lime juice and salt.

Per serving: 50 calories, 0 g fat, 1 g protein, 12 g carbohydrate, 0 mg cholesterol, 300 mg sodium

Cost: Per Recipe: $ 2.08; Per Serving: $ 0.52

Mexican Vegetable Salad

Serving Size: 1/2 cup
Yield: 7 servings

Ingredients:

1 cup cucumber, chopped, with peel
1 can (8 3/4 ounce) corn, drained
1 can (16 ounces) stewed tomatoes
2 Tablespoons chopped red pepper
2 Tablespoons chopped green pepper
2 Tablespoons red wine vinegar
1/2 teaspoon garlic powder
1/2 teaspoon ground cumin
1/4 teaspoon dried cilantro or coriander
1/8 teaspoon black pepper

Instructions:

1. Combine ingredients and mix well.

2. Serve cold.

Per serving: 50 calories, 0 g fat, 2 g protein, 12 g carbohydrate, 0 mg cholesterol, 320 mg sodium

Cost: Per Recipe: $ 1.79; Per Serving: $ 0.26

Egg Salad

Serving Size: 1/4 of recipe
Yield: 4 servings

Ingredients:

4 finely chopped hard boiled eggs
2 teaspoons pickle relish
1/2 teaspoon salt
1 teaspoon wet mustard
1/4 cup mayonnaise

Instructions:

1. Put the eggs in a pan of cold water. Bring to a boil, then lower heat and simmer for 15 minutes.

2. Cool promptly in cold water, then in refrigerator, so the eggs will be easy to shell.

3. Remove the shells from eggs, and chop the eggs finely.

4. Mix all the ingredients together.

Per serving: 140 calories, 14 g fat, 3 g protein, 1 g carbohydrate, 110 mg cholesterol, 440 mg sodium

Cost: Per Recipe: $ 0.79; Per Serving: $ 0.20

Country-Style Potato Salad

Serving Size: 1 cup
Yield: 4 servings

Ingredients:

3 medium baking potatoes
1 cup chopped celery
1/2 cup minced onion
1 cup frozen peas
1 Tablespoon prepared mustard
1/2 cup mayonnaise, low-fat
1/2 cup yogurt, nonfat plain
fresh cracked black pepper to taste
Garnish: lettuce and tomato

Instructions:

1. Wash potatoes, leave skin on and cut into bite-sized chunks.

2. Place in pan and cover with water. Bring to a boil, lower to simmer and cook uncovered until potatoes are tender, about 20 minutes.

3. Drain in colander and sprinkle lightly with cold water.

4. In the meantime, put the rest of the ingredients in a large mixing bowl. Drain potatoes well and add to the bowl.

5. Mix well and refrigerate until ready to use.

6. Garnish with fresh lettuce and sliced tomatoes.

Per serving: 180 calories, 10 g fat, 6 g protein, 18 g carbohydrate, 10 mg cholesterol, 330 mg sodium

Cost: Per Recipe: $ 2.69; Per Serving: $ 0.67

Herbed Potato Salad

Serving Size: 1/2 cup
Yield: 6 servings

Ingredients:

1 1/2 pounds quartered red potatoes
1/2 cup Italian dressing, light
1/2 Tablespoon mustard, spicy brown
1 Tablespoon chopped, fresh parsley
3/4 teaspoon garlic salt
1/4 teaspoon ground black pepper
1/2 cup chopped green bell pepper
1/2 cup chopped red bell pepper
1/2 cup sliced green onions

Instructions:

1. Cook potatoes in boiling water over high heat until tender, about 10 minutes.

2. Drain well and let cool.

3. Place potatoes in a medium bowl and set aside.

4. In a small bowl, combine dressing, mustard, parsley, and seasonings.

5. Pour mixture over potatoes and toss well.

6. Carefully stir in bell peppers and green onions.

7. Cover and chill until ready to serve.

Per serving: 120 calories, 2.5 g fat, 3 g protein, 22 g carbohydrate, 0 mg cholesterol, 340 mg sodium

Cost: Per Recipe: $ 2.44; Per Serving: $ 0.41

Pasta Salad

Serving Size: 1/2 cup
Yield: 12 servings

Ingredients:

3 cups pasta, uncooked
1/2 cup chopped celery
1 medium chopped bell pepper
1/2 cup diced carrots
1/2 cup chopped broccoli
1/3 cup mayonnaise
1 1/2 Tablespoon garlic powder
1/4 teaspoon black pepper

Instructions:

1. Cook pasta according to package directions.

2. Drain and place in bowl or pan.

3. Add the rest of the ingredients and mix well.

4. Chill in refrigerator before serving.

Per serving: 160 calories, 5 g fat, 4 g protein, 23 g carbohydrate, 0 mg cholesterol, 45 mg sodium

Cost: Per Recipe: $ 1.61; Per Serving: $ 0.13

Apple Salad

Serving Size: 1/2 cup
Yield: 8 servings

Ingredients:

2 cups diced apples
1 cup diced celery
1/2 cup raisins
1/2 cup nuts
2 Tablespoons salad dressing or mayonnaise
1 Tablespoon orange juice

Instructions:

1. Mix orange juice with salad dressing or mayonnaise.

2. Toss apples, celery, raisins and nuts with the dressing mixture.

Per serving: 110 calories, 6 g fat, 2 g protein, 15 g carbohydrate, 0 mg cholesterol, 45 mg sodium

Cost: Per Recipe: $ 1.78; Per Serving: $ 0.22

Apple Cranberry Salad

Serving Size: 1/8 of recipe
Yield: 8 servings

Ingredients:

1 head of lettuce (about 10 cups)
2 medium sliced apples
1/2 cup chopped walnuts
1 cup dried cranberries
1/2 cup sliced green onions
3/4 cup vinaigrette dressing

Instructions:

1. Toss lettuce, apples, walnuts, cranberries, and onions in large bowl.

2. Add dressing; toss to coat. Serve immediately.

Per serving: 140 calories, 5 g fat, 2 g protein, 24 g carbohydrate, 0 mg cholesterol, 10 mg sodium

Cost: Per Recipe: $ 4.02; Per Serving: $ 0.50

Fruit Salad

Serving Size: 1/2 cup
Yield: 14 servings

Ingredients:

1 can (16 ounce) drained fruit cocktail
2 sliced bananas
2 oranges cut into bite-sized pieces
2 apples cut into bite-sized pieces
8 ounces yogurt, low-fat, piña colada-flavored

Instructions:

1. Mix fruit in a large bowl.

2. Add yogurt and mix well.

3. Chill in refrigerator before serving.

Per serving: 70 calories, 0 g fat, 1 g protein, 17 g carbohydrate, 0 mg cholesterol, 10 mg sodium

Cost: Per Recipe: $ 3.12; Per Serving: $ 0.22

Oprah's Outtasight Salad

Serving Size: 1 cup
Yield: 4 servings

Ingredients:

2 cups salad greens of your choice
1 cup chopped vegetables (tomatoes, cucumbers,
carrots, green beans)
1 cup canned in juice pineapple chunks, drained or fresh
orange segments
1/4 cup Dynamite Dressing
2 Tablespoons raisins or dried cranberries
2 Tablespoons chopped nuts, any kind

Dynamite Dressing Ingredients:
1/4 cup yogurt, nonfat, fruit-flavored
1 Tablespoon orange juice
1 1/2 teaspoon white vinegar

Instructions:

1. Put mixed salad greens on a large platter or in a salad
bowl.

2. In a large bowl, mix chopped vegetables and orange
segments. Add dressing and stir. Spoon mixture over
salad greens.

3. Top with raisins and nuts. Serve.

Dynamite Dressing Preparation:

1. In a small bowl, mix all ingredients. Refrigerate until
ready to serve.

Per serving: 100 calories, 2.5 g fat, 2 g protein, 18 g
carbohydrate, 0 mg cholesterol, 30 mg sodium

Cost: Per Recipe: $ 1.70; Per Serving: $ 0.42

Chicken Salad

Serving Size: 1/6 of recipe
Yield: 6 servings

Ingredients:

2 1/2 cups cooked, diced chicken breast
1/2 cup chopped celery
1/4 cup chopped onion
2 Tablespoons pickle relish
1/2 cup light mayonnaise

Instructions:

1. Combine all ingredients.

2. Refrigerate until ready to serve.

3. Use within 1-2 days. Chicken salad does not freeze well.

How to use:

1. Make chicken salad sandwiches.

2. Make a pasta salad by mixing with 2 cups cooked pasta.

3. Kids will love this salad served in a tomato or a cucumber boat.

Per serving: 160 calories, 8 g fat, 17 g protein, 4 g carbohydrate, 50 mg cholesterol, 220 mg sodium

Cost: Per Recipe: $ 4.56; Per Serving: $ 0.76

Crunchy Chicken Salad

Serving Size: 3/4 cup
Yield: 5 servings

Ingredients:

2 cups chunked cooked chicken
1/2 cup celery
1/4 cup green pepper
1/4 onion
1/2 cucumber
1/2 cup grapes
1 small diced apple (leave the peel on)
1/4 cup yogurt, plain

Instructions:

1. Use leftover cooked chicken, or cook enough chicken to make 2 cups of chicken pieces.

2. Chop the celery into small pieces.

3. Chop the green pepper into small pieces.

4. Peel and chop 1/4 of an onion.

5. Peel and chop half of a cucumber.

6. Chop the apple into pieces. It's okay to leave the peel on the apple.

7. Cut the grapes in half.

8. Put all the ingredients in a large bowl. Stir together.

Note: Serve on lettuce, crackers, or bread.

Per serving: 140 calories, 4.5 g fat, 17 g protein, 9 g carbohydrate, 50 mg cholesterol, 65 mg sodium

Cost: Per Recipe: $ 3.14; Per Serving: $ 0.63

Chicken Rice Salad

Serving Size: 2 cups
Yield: 4 servings

Ingredients:

4 cups lettuce
2 cups brown rice, cooked
2 cups chicken breast, skinless roasted
1 cored and diced tomato
1 cored and diced green pepper
1 Tablespoon olive oil
1 juice of one lemon
2 Tablespoons vinegar, flavored
dash hot pepper sauce (optional)
Italian herb mix and black pepper to taste, (optional)

Instructions:

1. Toss all ingredients together in a large salad bowl.

2. Use personal taste preferences to determine the amounts of seasonings.

3. Serve immediately. This salad looks great when served on a large plate with a few of the seasonings sprinkled on top.

Per serving: 280 calories, 7 g fat, 25 g protein, 28 g carbohydrate, 60 mg cholesterol, 65 mg sodium

Cost: Per Recipe: $ 6.56; Per Serving: $ 1.64

Turkey Salad with Orange Vinaigrette

Serving Size: 1 1/2 cups
Yield: 4 servings

Ingredients:

1/4 cup orange juice
2 Tablespoons vinegar, white wine
2 Tablespoons finely chopped onion
1/4 teaspoon salt
dash of pepper
1 Tablespoon oil
2 teaspoons Dijon mustard
4 cups torn salad greens
2 cups cooked turkey breast, cut into julienne strips
1 can (11 ounce) drained mandarin orange segments
1/2 cup sliced celery

Instructions:

1. In a jar with tight-fitting lid, combine all vinaigrette ingredients; shake well. Alternatively, place ingredients in a small mixing bowl and mix together with a whisk.

2. In large bowl, combine all salad ingredients; toss gently.

3. Serve with vinaigrette. If desired, garnish with fresh strawberries.

Notes: You can substitute 1 1/2 teaspoons dried chopped onion for the chopped fresh onion. Prepare the dressing at least 10 minutes before you need it to allow the dried onion to rehydrate from the fluids in the dressing.

Another way to add crunch to your salad would be to use 4 tablespoons chopped walnuts instead of the celery.

Per serving: 200 calories, 6 g fat, 23 g protein, 13 g carbohydrate, 50 mg cholesterol, 280 mg sodium

Cost: Per Recipe: $ 3.98; Per Serving: $ 0.99

Tuna, Green Beans and Macaroni Salad

Serving Size: 1/8 of recipe
Yield: 8 servings

Ingredients:

14 ounce package elbow macaroni
1 can (16 ounce) drained green beans or other
vegetable
1 can (7 ounce) tuna packed in water, drained and
flaked
1 cup diced cheese
1/2 cup diced sweet pickles
1/2 cup diced onions
1 cup yogurt, plain
1/2 cup light mayonnaise
1 1/2 Tablespoons lemon juice
1/4 teaspoon salt
1/4 teaspoon seasoned pepper

Instructions:

1. Prepare elbow macaroni according to package
directions and drain.

2. Add vegetables, tuna, onions, cheese, and pickles.

3. Mix yogurt, salad dressing, lemon juice, salt and
seasoned pepper.

4. Toss with macaroni mixture.

5. Chill before serving.

Per serving: 360 calories, 12 g fat, 18 g protein, 47 g
carbohydrate, 30 mg cholesterol, 550 mg sodium

Cost: Per Recipe: $ 4.64; Per Serving: $ 0.58

Tuna Apple Salad

Serving Size: 1/2 pita
Yield: 4 servings

Ingredients:

1 can (12 ounces) tuna, packed in water
2 Tablespoons minced red onion
1 cored and chopped apple
1 cup chopped celery
1 cup golden raisins
5 Tablespoons Italian dressing, light
2 cups salad greens
2 pita breads, cut in half

Instructions:

1. In a small bowl, stir together tuna, onion, apple, celery, raisins, and 2 Tablespoons of dressing.

2. In another bowl, toss together salad greens with remaining dressing.

3. Carefully open pita breads and fill with equal amounts of greens and tuna salad.

Per serving: 270 calories, 4 g fat, 26 g protein, 32 g carbohydrate, 25 mg cholesterol, 360 mg sodium

Cost: Per Recipe: $ 4.48; Per Serving: $ 1.12

Caribbean Bean Salad

Serving Size: 1 cup
Yield: 4 servings

Ingredients:

4 cups chopped romaine lettuce
1/4 cup red onion
1 cup canned, drained and rinsed, black beans
1 peeled and diced orange
1 diced tomato
1 Tablespoon olive oil
3 Tablespoons red wine vinegar
1 teaspoon dried oregano
black pepper to taste

Instructions:

1. Toss all ingredients together in large salad bowl.

2. Serve immediately or refrigerate up to one hour.

Per serving: 100 calories, 4 g fat, 4 g protein, 17 g carbohydrate, 0 mg cholesterol, 270 mg sodium

Cost: Per Recipe: $ 1.99; Per Serving: $ 0.50

Black Bean and Rice Salad

Serving Size: 1 cup
Yield: 3 servings

Ingredients:

1/2 cup chopped onion
1/2 cup chopped green or red bell pepper
1 cup cooked and cooled brown or white rice
1 can (15 ounce) drained and rinsed black beans

Dressing:
1/4 cup rice vinegar or white wine vinegar or lemon juice
1/2 teaspoon dry mustard powder (optional)
1 chopped clove garlic or 1/2 teaspoon garlic powder
1/2 teaspoon salt
1/4 teaspoon pepper
2 Tablespoons vegetable oil

Instructions:

1. In a mixing bowl, stir together onion, red or green pepper, rice and beans.

2. In a jar with a tight fitting lid, add vinegar, dry mustard, garlic, salt, pepper and vegetable oil. Shake until dressing is evenly mixed.

3. Pour dressing over bean mixture and stir to mix evenly. Chill for at least one hour. Serve cold as a side dish or main dish.

Per serving: 290 calories, 11 g fat, 10 g protein, 38 g carbohydrate, 0 mg cholesterol, 830 mg sodium

Cost: Per Recipe: $ 1.58; Per Serving: $ 0.53

Tofu Salad

Serving Size: 1/2 cup
Yield: 8 servings

Ingredients:

1 pound firm tofu
1/2 cup diced scallions
1/2 cup diced celery
1/2 cup diced carrots
2 Tablespoons yellow mustard
1/2 teaspoon turmeric
1 teaspoon onion powder
1 teaspoon garlic powder
1/2 cup low-fat mayonnaise

Instructions:

1. Drain tofu. Wrap in layers of paper towels to dry.

2. Place a heavy object on top of tofu (like a skillet) and let it sit while you prepare other ingredients.

3. Wash and dice vegetables, if desired.

4. Mash tofu well with fork. Stir in spices and mayonnaise. Then gently stir in vegetables.

5. Use as a sandwich spread or serve on a bed of crisp greens.

Note: Use a variety of chopped vegetables for different flavors and textures.

Per serving: 100 calories, 7 g fat, 5 g protein, 4 g carbohydrate, 5 mg cholesterol, 160 mg sodium

Cost: Per Recipe: $ 3.04; Per Serving: $ 0.38

SNaCKS

Deviled Eggs

Serving Size: 1 egg (2 filled halves)
Yield: 6 servings

Ingredients:

6 large hard-boiled and peeled eggs
1/4 cup mayonnaise
1/8 teaspoon salt
1/8 teaspoon pepper

Instructions:

1. Hard boil eggs by placing eggs in a saucepan and covering them with water. Bring to a boil. Reduce heat to simmer; cook for 15 minutes.

2. Immediately rinse under cold water to stop cooking and to make it easy to peel off shells. Refrigerate peeled eggs (without shells) until ready for use.

3. Slice eggs into halves lengthwise. Remove yellow yolks and save whites.

4. Place yolks in a one quart zip lock style bag along with the remaining ingredients (except the egg whites). Press out air.

5. Close bag and knead (mush together) until ingredients are well-blended. (Note: you could also put yolks in a bowl with other ingredients [except the egg whites], and mix together well until they look like a paste).

6. Push contents toward one corner of the bag. Cut about 1/2 inch off the corner of the bag. Squeezing the bag gently, fill reserved egg white hollows with the yolk mixture. (Note if you used a bowl, you can spoon the yolk mixture into the egg whites).

7. Chill to blend flavors.

Per serving: 140 calories, 12 g fat, 6 g protein, 0 g carbohydrate, 215 mg cholesterol, 170 mg sodium

Cost: Per Recipe: $ 0.75; Per Serving: $ 0.12

Baked Chicken Nuggets

Serving Size: 1/4 of recipe
Yield: 4 servings

Ingredients:

1 1/2 pounds chicken thighs, boneless, skinless
1 cup cereal crumbs, cornflake type
1/2 teaspoon Italian herb seasoning
1/4 teaspoon garlic powder
1/4 teaspoon onion powder
1 teaspoon paprika

Instructions:

1. Preheat oven to 400 degrees. Lightly grease a cooking sheet.

2. Remove skin and bone from chicken thighs*; cut thighs into bite-sized pieces.

3. Place cornflakes in plastic bag and crush by using a rolling pin.

4. Add remaining ingredients to crushed cornflakes. Close bag tightly and shake until blended.

5. Add a few chicken pieces at a time to crumb mixture. Shake to coat evenly.

6. Place chicken pieces on cooking sheet so they are not touching.

7. Bake until golden brown, about 12-14 minutes.

*Note: To remove bone from chicken thigh: Place chicken on cutting board. Remove skin from thighs. Turn chicken thighs over. Cut around bone and remove it.

Per serving: 230 calories, 7 g fat, 34 g protein, 7 g carbohydrate, 140 mg cholesterol, 240 mg sodium

Cost: Per Recipe: $ 3.82; Per Serving: $ 0.96

Granola Bars

Serving Size: 1 bar
Yield: 24 servings

Ingredients:

1 cup honey
1 cup peanut butter
3 1/2 cups rolled oats
1/2 cup raisins
1/2 cup grated carrots
1/2 cup coconut

Instructions:

1. Preheat oven to 350 degrees.

2. Peel and grate the carrots.

3. Put the honey and peanut butter in a large saucepan. Cook on low heat until they melt.

4. Remove the pan from the heat. Turn off the burner.

5. Add oatmeal, raisins, carrots, and coconut to the saucepan. Stir well, and let it cool until you can safely touch it with your hands.

6. Put the mix in the baking pan. Press the mix firmly into the bottom of the pan.

7. Bake for 25 minutes.

8. Cut into 24 bars.

Per serving: 160 calories, 6 g fat, 4 g protein, 25 g carbohydrate, 0 mg cholesterol, 5 mg sodium

Cost: Per Recipe: $ 5.72; Per Serving: $ 0.24

Anytime Pizza

Serving Size: 1 slice of bread
Yield: 2 servings

Ingredients:

1/2 loaf Italian or French bread split lengthwise, or 2
split English muffins
1/2 cup pizza sauce
1/2 cup cheese, low-fat shredded mozzarella or cheddar
3 Tablespoons chopped green pepper
3 Tablespoons sliced mushrooms, fresh or canned
other vegetable toppings as desired (optional)
Italian seasoning (optional)

Instructions:

1. Toast the bread or English muffin until slightly brown.

2. Top bread or muffin with pizza sauce, vegetables and
low-fat cheese.

3. Sprinkle with Italian seasonings as desired.

4. Return bread to toaster oven (or regular oven
preheated to 350 degrees).

5. Heat until cheese melts.

Per serving: 180 calories, 7 g fat, 12 g protein, 21 g
carbohydrate, 15 mg cholesterol, 540 mg sodium

Cost: Per Recipe: $ 1.98; Per Serving: $ 0.99

Veggie Stuffed Pita

Serving Size: 1/12 of recipe
Yield: 12 servings

Ingredients:

2 medium (2 1/2 cups chopped) zucchini
4 medium (1 1/4 cups grated) carrots
2 cups chopped broccoli
12 ounces cheddar cheese, low-fat
1/2 teaspoon oregano
1/4 teaspoon black pepper
1/4 teaspoon garlic powder
1/4 teaspoon onion powder
2 Tablespoons vegetable oil
12 - 6 inch mini-pitas

Instructions:

1. Wash vegetables.

2. Remove the broccoli flowers from stems, cut the flowers into small florets and put into mixing bowl.

3. Peel carrots and cut off the ends. Grate carrots and put into mixing bowl.

4. Slice the zucchini into thin slices. Cut each slice into quarters and put into bowl.

5. Grate the cheese and put into a separate bowl.

6. Measure oregano, pepper, garlic powder, onion powder and mix together.

7. Heat oil in a skillet. Put the spices in the heated oil and then add the mixture of vegetables to the pan. Stir vegetables with a wooden spoon and sauté about 5 minutes. When the vegetables are slightly tender, remove from heat.

8. Spoon vegetable mixture into the pita. Top the hot vegetables with 1 ounce grated cheese.

Note: Substitute green pepper, mushrooms or onions in place of listed vegetables.

Per serving: 250 calories, 5 g fat, 13 g protein, 37 g carbohydrate, 5 mg cholesterol, 510 mg sodium

Cost: Per Recipe: $ 8.02; Per Serving: $ 0.67

Peanut Butter and Fruit-wich

Serving Size: 1 open-faced sandwich
Yield: 1 serving

Ingredients:

1 slice whole wheat bread
2 Tablespoons peanut butter
1/4 thinly sliced apple or banana
2 Tablespoons sliced or grated carrot (optional)

Instructions:

1. Spread 2 Tablespoons peanut butter on bread.

2. Place fruit slices on top.

3. Optional: Top with grated carrot.

Notes: Instead of whole wheat bread try crunchy graham crackers or roll up the filling in a soft tortilla. Instead of fresh fruit use canned, drained pineapple.

Per serving: 270 calories, 17 g fat, 11 g protein, 24 g carbohydrate, 0 mg cholesterol, 150 mg sodium

Cost: Per Recipe: $ 0.27; Per Serving: $ 0.27

Cracker Funny Face

Serving Size: 1 cracker
Yield: 1 serving

Ingredients:

1 Tablespoon peanut butter
1 large graham cracker or use whole grain or saltine crackers
1 Tablespoon shredded cheddar cheese
3-4 raisins
2 large green peas
1 grape cut in half

Instructions:

1. Spread peanut butter on a cracker in the shape of a face.

2. Sprinkle grated cheese at top for hair.

3. Place raisins on cracker for mouth.

4. Use peas for eyes and 1/2 grape for nose.

Note: This snack is intended for children over age two. Do not serve to younger children who may choke.

Per serving: 190 calories, 12 g fat, 7 g protein, 16 g carbohydrate, 5 mg cholesterol, 110 mg sodium

Cost: Per Recipe: $ 0.23; Per Serving: $ 0.23

Microwave-Baked Apple

Serving Size: 1 apple
Yield: 4 servings

Ingredients:

4 large baking apples
1/2 cup brown sugar
1 teaspoon cinnamon

Instructions:

1. Wash apples in clear running water and then remove core.

2. Cut a thin slice off bottom of each apple to form a flat surface. Place apples in a microwave safe baking dish. Arrange the apples around the outside edge of the dish for more even cooking in the microwave.

3. Mix brown sugar and cinnamon in a small dish. Spoon mixture into center of apples.

4. Cover apples with wax paper and microwave on high power 6 to 10 minutes or until apples are soft.

Notes: One pound apples = 3 medium = 3 cups sliced. This is good information to know at the grocery store.

Favorite varieties of apples for baking are Jonathan, Granny Smith, Braeburn and Golden Delicious. Any tart apple works well.

If you have apples left, keep in the fridge for a handy snack later on.

Per serving: 220 calories, 0 g fat, 1 g protein, 57 g carbohydrate, 0 mg cholesterol, 15 mg sodium

Cost: Per Recipe: $ 2.70; Per Serving: $ 0.67

Fruit Kabobs

Serving Size: 1/8 of recipe
Yield: 8 servings

Ingredients:

1 cup watermelon chunks
1 cup pineapple chunks
1 cup grapes, red seedless
1 cup stemmed strawberries
2 kiwis peeled and cut in quarters
8 - 6 inches long bamboo skewers
1 cup yogurt, nonfat, strawberry-flavored

Instructions:

1. Place fruit chunks on bamboo skewers. Place fruit kabobs on platter.

2. Place nonfat strawberry yogurt in bowl. Serve kabobs with yogurt on the side.

Per serving: 60 calories, 0 g fat, 2 g protein, 14 g carbohydrate, 0 mg cholesterol, 20 mg sodium

Cost: Per Recipe: $ 2.86; Per Serving: $ 0.36

Vegetable Medley with Salsa Dip

Serving Size: 1 cup vegetables and 1/2 cup salsa
Yield: 4 servings

Ingredients:

2 carrots, cut into 3-inch sticks
2 celery stalks, cut into 3-inch sticks
1/2 jicama, peeled and cut into 3-inch sticks
1 bunch radishes, trimmed
6 green onions, trimmed
1 cup fat free sour cream
1 cup Fresh Salsa

Fresh Salsa Ingredients:
2 chopped tomatoes
1/2 chopped onion
3 finely chopped jalapeño chilies, seeded if desired
1/4 cup chopped fresh cilantro
1/4 teaspoon salt
juice of 1 lime

Instructions:

1. Arrange vegetables on a platter.

2. In a small bowl, mix sour cream and salsa. Serve.

Fresh Salsa Preparation:

1. In a medium bowl, mix all ingredients.

2. Serve or store salsa in refrigerator for up to three days in a covered plastic or glass container.

Safety Tip: Caution: When handling hot peppers, the oils can cause burning and skin irritation. You can wear clean kitchen gloves or wash hands thoroughly after preparing. KEEP HANDS AWAY FROM EYES.

Per serving: 150 calories, 0.5 g fat, 5 g protein, 30 g carbohydrate, 10 mg cholesterol, 290 mg sodium

Cost: Per Recipe: $ 6.08; Per Serving: $ 1.52

Pretzel Shapes

Serving Size: 1 pretzel
Yield: 12 servings

Ingredients:

1 package dry yeast
1/2 cup warm water
1 teaspoon honey
1 1/3 cups flour
1 teaspoon salt

Instructions:

1. Preheat oven to 425 degrees.

2. In a small bowl, dissolve yeast in warm water, add honey and let set for a few minutes.

3. In a large mixing bowl, measure flour and salt.

4. Add yeast mixture to flour mixture and stir until it forms a smooth ball. Add a little more flour if the dough is sticky.

5. Knead dough on countertop or dough board until it forms a smooth ball. Add a little flour if the dough is sticky.

6. Divide dough into 12 pieces about the size of a walnut. Roll each ball into a snake and then twist to make a pretzel, letter or other fun shape.

7. Place pretzels on a baking sheet lightly coated with cooking spray. Bake for 10 to 12 minutes until golden brown.

Per serving: 50 calories, 0 g fat, 2 g protein, 11 g carbohydrate, 0 mg cholesterol, 190 mg sodium

Cost: Per Recipe: $ 0.65; Per Serving: $ 0.05

Tortilla Chips and Bean Dip

Serving Size: 8 pieces
Yield: 4 servings

Ingredients:

4 corn tortillas
1 can (16 ounce) kidney beans
1/4 cup salsa
1/4 cup sour cream, nonfat
1/2 cup shredded cheddar cheese
1 cup shredded lettuce

Instructions:

1. Preheat oven to 400 degrees.

2. Place tortillas in a stack on cutting board. With a sharp knife, cut stack into eight pieces, forming triangles or wedges.

3. Lay tortilla pieces out in single layer on baking sheet. Set aside while making dip.

4. Open can of beans. Pour beans in colander; rinse and drain. Place beans in a small mixing bowl and mash with a potato masher. Spread beans over bottom of baking dish.

5. Measure salsa and spread over beans.

6. Measure sour cream and spread over beans.

7. Grate and measure cheese; sprinkle over bean mixture.

8. Place lettuce wedge on cutting board. Slice into thin strips; set aside.

9. Place both the baking sheet with tortilla pieces and the dip in preheated oven. Bake about 8 minutes or until tortilla pieces are crisp and dip is bubbly. Sprinkle lettuce over dip and serve with tortilla chips.

Create-a-Flavor Changes:
- Use Monterey Jack or another cheese.
- Substitute black beans for kidney beans.
- Substitute 1/4 cup chopped fresh tomatoes for taco sauce.
- Spread one small can chopped green chilies over beans.

Per serving: 290 calories, 5 g fat, 12 g protein, 55 g carbohydrate, 5 mg cholesterol, 550 mg sodium

Cost: Per Recipe: $ 2.24; Per Serving: $ 0.56

BreaDS & MUFFINS

Banana Bread

Serving Size: 1 slice
Yield: 12 servings

Ingredients:

3 large well-ripened bananas
1 egg
2 Tablespoons vegetable oil
1/3 cup milk
1/3 cup sugar
1 teaspoon salt
1 teaspoon baking soda
1/2 teaspoon baking powder
1 1/2 cup flour

Instructions:

1. Preheat the oven to 350 degrees.

2. Peel the bananas. Put them in a mixing bowl. Mash the bananas with a fork.

3. Add the egg, oil, milk, sugar, salt, baking soda, and baking powder. Mix well with the fork.

4. Slowly stir the flour into the banana mixture. Stir for 20 seconds until the flour is moistened.

5. Lightly grease the bread pan with a little oil -OR- cooking spray -OR- line it with wax paper.

6. Pour the batter into the bread pan.

7. Bake for 45 minutes until a toothpick inserted near the middle comes out clean.

8. Let the bread cool for 5 minutes before removing it from the pan.

Notes: The key to good banana bread is to use well-ripened bananas that are covered with brown speckles. Try using half whole wheat flour to add some fiber.

Per serving: 140 calories, 3 g fat, 3 g protein, 26 g carbohydrate, 20 mg cholesterol, 330 mg sodium

Cost: Per Recipe: $ 0.97; Per Serving: $ 0.08

Blueberry Muffins

Serving Size: 1 muffin
Yield: 12 servings

Ingredients:

1/2 cup vegetable oil
1 cup sugar
2 eggs
1/2 cups low-fat milk
1 teaspoon vanilla
2 cup flour
2 teaspoons baking powder
1/2 teaspoon salt
2 cups blueberries (fresh or frozen)

Instructions:

1. Preheat the oven to 375 degrees.

2. Grease the muffin pans.

3. In a large mixing bowl, stir the oil and sugar until creamy.

4. Add eggs, milk and vanilla. Mix until blended.

5. In a medium mixing bowl, stir together the flour, baking powder, and salt.

6. Add the flour mix to the oil and sugar in the large bowl. Stir together.

7. Stir the blueberries into the batter.

8. Fill each muffin cup 2/3 full with batter.

9. Bake for 25 to 30 minutes.

Per serving: 250 calories, 11 g fat, 4 g protein, 37 g carbohydrate, 35 mg cholesterol, 200 mg sodium

Cost: Per Recipe: $ 2.58; Per Serving: $ 0.21

Bran Muffins

Serving Size: 2 muffins
Yield: 30 servings

Ingredients:

5 cups flour
2 teaspoons salt
2 teaspoons baking soda
3 cups sugar
1 box (15 ounces) raisin bran (8 cups)
4 eggs beaten
4 cups buttermilk
1 cup oil
vegetable spray or oil

Instructions:

1. Preheat oven to 425 degrees.

2. Measure flour into 1 gallon container. Add salt, soda, sugar and raisin bran to the flour and mix well with spoon.

3. With a spoon, make a "well" in the center of the dry ingredients.

4. In the medium size bowl, beat the eggs with a fork until whites and yolk are evenly blended.

5. Add milk and oil to eggs. Beat with fork.

6. Add liquid to dry ingredients. Stir until dry ingredients are moistened (mixture will be lumpy).

7. Lightly oil the bottoms of the paper cups in the muffin pan (or use muffin cups). Fill the muffin cups to 3/4 full.

8. Bake for 15-20 minutes. After baking, the muffins can be frozen for future use.

Per serving: 290 calories, 9 g fat, 5 g protein, 50 g carbohydrate, 30 mg cholesterol, 380 mg sodium

Cost: Per Recipe: $ 5.82; Per Serving: $ 0.19

Chapati Flatbread

Serving Size: 1 flatbread
Yield: 6 servings

Ingredients:

2 cups whole wheat flour
2/3 cup warm water
2 teaspoons vegetable oil
pinch of salt

Instructions:

1. Place the flour in a large mixing bowl. Add water, oil, and salt. Mix with fork and then with hands. Keep mixing until you can make a ball.

2. Knead the dough for about 10 minutes. Let rest for 30 minutes in the bowl, covered with a damp cloth.

3. Roll the ball into a 12-inch log and cut into 6 chunks.

4. Roll each chunk into a very thin pancake, about 7-inches in diameter. Don't worry about making the dough into a perfect circle-just try to get it as thin as you can.

5. Heat a cast iron skillet (lightly greased) on medium-high heat. Place one chapati in the skillet and cook for 30 seconds.

6. Use a spatula to lift bread. When chapati gets brown spots and bubbles, flip it over and cook for another 30 seconds.

7..Wrap the cooked chapati in a cloth napkin while cooking the rest.

8. Eat them right away with a little butter or margarine, or use as scoops for eating other dishes.

Per serving: 150 calories, 2.5 g fat, 5 g protein, 29 g carbohydrate, 0 mg cholesterol, 50 mg sodium

Cost: Per Recipe: $ 0.48; Per Serving: $ 0.08

Oatmeal Raisin Muffins

Serving Size: 1 muffin
Yield: 12 servings

Ingredients:

1 egg
1 cup milk
1/3 cup oil
1 1/4 cups flour
1 cup oatmeal
1/3 cup sugar
1 teaspoon baking powder
1 teaspoon salt
1/2 cup raisins
margarine or butter (to grease muffin cups)

Instructions:

1. Preheat the oven to 400 degrees.

2. Put the egg, milk, and oil in a small mixing bowl. Slowly stir them together.

3. In a large mixing bowl, add the flour, oatmeal, sugar, baking powder, salt and raisins. Stir until they are mixed.

4. Pour the egg-milk-oil mix into the medium bowl with the dry ingredients. Stir until the dry ingredients are barely moistened. Do not over-mix (the batter should be lumpy).

5. Grease each cup in the muffin pans with some margarine or butter. Spoon the batter into the cups in each muffin pan, until each cup is half-full with batter.

6. Bake for 20 to 25 minutes, or until the muffins are golden brown.

Per serving: 180 calories, 7 g fat, 4 g protein, 27 g carbohydrate, 20 mg cholesterol, 330 mg sodium

Cost: Per Recipe: $ 1.49; Per Serving: $ 0.12

Corn Bread

Serving Size: 2-inch square
Yield: 12 servings

Ingredients:

1 cup cornmeal
1 cup all purpose flour
2 Tablespoons sugar
1 Tablespoon baking powder
1 egg
1/4 cup vegetable oil
1 cup skim milk

Instructions:

1. Heat oven to 425 degrees. Grease 8- or 9-inch square pan.

2. Measure cornmeal, flour, sugar, and baking powder into a large mixing bowl. Stir to combine ingredients.

3. Crack egg into a small bowl and beat with a fork to combine white and yolk.

4. Add egg, oil, and milk to flour mixture. Mix until ingredients are well blended.

5. Pour batter into prepared pan.

6. Bake 20 to 25 minutes, until firm to touch or wooden pick inserted in the center comes out clean.

Note: For Corn Bread Muffins, pour batter into prepared muffin cups. Bake 20 minutes at 400 degrees.

Create-a-Flavor Changes:

Buttermilk Corn Bread. Use only 2 teaspoons baking powder and add 1/4 teaspoon baking soda. Substitute 1 cup buttermilk for skim milk.

Corny Corn Bread. Add 1 cup kernels (fresh, frozen, or canned, well drained) with the milk.

Cheesy Corn Bread. Add 1/2 cup shredded cheddar cheese with the milk.

Chili Cheese Corn Bread. Add 1/2 teaspoon chili powder to the flour mixture. Drain one 4-ounce can chopped green chilies. Add chilies and 1/4 cup shredded Monterey jack cheese with the milk.

Per serving: 140 calories, 5 g fat, 3 g protein, 20 g carbohydrate, 20 mg cholesterol, 140 mg sodium

Cost: Per Recipe: $ 0.91; Per Serving: $ 0.08

Mixed Grain Bread

Serving Size: 1 slice
Yield: 20 servings

Ingredients:

1/4 cup yellow cornmeal
1/4 cup packed brown sugar
1 teaspoon salt
2 Tablespoons vegetable oil
1 cup boiling water
1 package active dry yeast
1/4 cup warm (105 - 115 degrees) water
1/3 cup whole wheat flour
1/4 cup rye flour
2 1/4 - 2 3/4 cup all purpose flour

Instructions:

1. Preheat oven to 375 degrees.

2. Mix cornmeal, brown sugar, salt and oil with boiling water, cool to lukewarm (105 - 115 degrees).

3. Dissolve yeast in 1/4 cup warm water; stir into cornmeal mixture. Add whole wheat and rye flours and mix well. Stir in enough all purpose flour to make dough stiff enough to knead.

4. Turn dough onto lightly floured surface. Knead until smooth and elastic, about 5 to 10 minutes.

5. Place dough in lightly oiled bowl, turning oil top. Cover with clean towel; let rise in warm place until double, about 1 hour.

6. Punch dough down; turn onto clean surface. Cover with clean towel; let rest 10 minutes. Shape dough and place in greased 9 x 5 inch pan. Cover with clean towel; let rise until almost double, about 1 hour.

7. Bake 35 to 45 minutes or until bread sounds hollow when tapped. Cover with aluminum foil during baking if

bread is browning too quickly. Remove bread from pan and cool on wire rack.

Per serving: 90 calories, 1.5 g fat, 2 g protein, 17 g carbohydrate, 0 mg cholesterol, 120 mg sodium

Cost: Per Recipe: $ 0.98; Per Serving: $ 0.05

Whole Wheat Muffins

Serving Size: 1 muffin
Yield: 12 servings

Ingredients:

1 cup all purpose flour
1 cup whole wheat flour
1/2 teaspoon salt
2 teaspoons baking powder
1/4 cup firmly packed brown sugar or white sugar
1 cup milk
2 eggs
1 teaspoon vanilla (optional)
1/4 cup melted margarine or butter or 1/4 cup vegetable oil
Topping:
1 Tablespoon sugar
1/2 teaspoon ground cinnamon

Instructions:

1. Preheat oven to 400 degrees.

2. Lightly oil or coat with non-stick spray the cups of a 12 cup muffin pan, or use paper muffin cups.

3. Mix together sugar and cinnamon for topping and set aside.

4. In a large bowl, stir together flour, salt, baking powder and sugar. In a glass or plastic liquid measuring cup, measure milk, then add eggs, vanilla (if using), and melted shortening or oil. Mix with a fork until egg is well combined with other ingredients.

5. Pour milk mixture over flour mixture and stir with a spoon, about 20 strokes, until flour is just moistened. Batter will be lumpy and thick.

6. Fill prepared muffin cups about 2/3 full with batter. Sprinkle about 1/4 teaspoon of cinnamon/sugar topping over each muffin.

7. Bake in oven for 20 to 25 minutes until golden brown. Serve warm. Leftovers may be frozen.

Per serving: 150 calories, 5 g fat, 4 g protein, 22 g carbohydrate, 35 mg cholesterol, 230 mg sodium

Cost: Per Recipe: $ 0.83; Per Serving: $ 0.07

Pumpkin Bread

Serving Size: 1 slice
Yield: 32 servings

Ingredients:

1 can (15 ounce) pumpkin
1 cup sugar
1/4 cup vegetable oil
1 cup yogurt, plain, low-fat
1 1/2 cups all purpose flour
1 1/2 cups whole wheat flour
2 teaspoons baking powder
2 teaspoons baking soda
2 teaspoons cinnamon
1/2 teaspoon salt
1 cup raisins

Instructions:

1. Preheat oven to 350 degrees.

2. In a large mixing bowl, beat together pumpkin, sugar, oil, and yogurt.

3. In a medium bowl, combine the flours, baking powder, soda, cinnamon, and salt; add to pumpkin mixture, stirring until just moistened.

4. Stir in raisins.

5. Pour into 2 greased 9x5x3 inch loaf pans and bake for about 1 hour.

6. Cool on a wire rack for 10 minutes; remove from pan and cool completely.

Note: Substituting yogurt for eggs and oil reduces fat and cholesterol.

Per serving: 110 calories, 2 g fat, 2 g protein, 21 g carbohydrate, 0 mg cholesterol, 150 mg sodium

Cost: Per Recipe: $ 2.90; Per Serving: $ 0.09

Peanut Butter Bread

Serving Size: 1 slice
Yield: 10 servings

Ingredients:

2 eggs
1 1/2 cup milk
1/3 cup granulated sugar
1 cup peanut butter
1 3/4 cups all purpose flour
1 Tablespoon baking powder
1/2 teaspoon salt

Instructions:

1. Preheat oven to 350 degrees.

2. Lightly grease or spray with non-stick spray, a loaf pan.

3. In large bowl, beat eggs. Add milk, sugar and peanut butter. Mix well.

4. In a separate bowl combine flour, baking powder, and salt. Mix thoroughly.

5. Add dry ingredients to wet ingredients. Mix only enough to moisten all ingredients.

6. Pour into prepared pan. (Pan will be half full). Bake for 1 hour.

Per serving: 260 calories, 14 g fat, 11 g protein, 24 g carbohydrate, 45 mg cholesterol, 300 mg sodium

Cost: Per Recipe: $ 1.71; Per Serving: $ 0.17

Zucchini Bread

Serving Size: 1 slice
Yield: 16 servings

Ingredients:

3 eggs
1 cup sugar
1/4 cup vegetable oil
2 cups grated zucchini
1 teaspoon vanilla
1 1/2 cups all purpose flour
1 1/2 cups whole wheat flour
1 teaspoon salt
2 teaspoons baking soda
2 teaspoons cinnamon
1/2 teaspoon baking powder
1/2 cup raisins

Instructions:

1. Preheat oven to 325 degrees.

2. Lightly grease and flour a 9 x 5 loaf pan.

3. In a large mixing bowl, beat eggs lightly. Add sugar, oil, zucchini, and vanilla and beat.

4. In a separate bowl, measure dry ingredients and stir to combine. Add nuts and raisins, if desired.

5. Add dry ingredients to the egg mixture. Stir just until all ingredients are moistened.

6. Spoon into loaf pan.

7. Bake for 50 minutes. Test for doneness by inserting a toothpick in the center. It should come out dry.

8. Allow loaf to cool 5 to 10 minutes before turning out onto a cooling rack.

9. Serve warm or allow to cool before slicing.

Per serving: 190 calories, 5 g fat, 4 g protein, 35 g carbohydrate, 40 mg cholesterol, 330 mg sodium

Cost: Per Recipe: $ 2.15; Per Serving: $ 0.13

Fruit Muffins

Serving Size: 1 muffin
Yield: 9 servings

Ingredients:

1 1/4 cups flour
1/4 cup sugar
1 teaspoon baking powder
1/2 teaspoon baking soda
3/4 cup buttermilk, low-fat
2 Tablespoons melted margarine
1 slightly beaten egg
1/2 teaspoon vanilla extract
1 cup coarsely chopped frozen strawberries or other fruit, fresh or frozen

Instructions:

1. Preheat oven to 400 degrees.

2. Spray muffin tin with nonstick cooking spray.

3. In a large bowl, combine the flour, sugar, baking powder, and baking soda. Stir well until all ingredients are blended.

4. In another bowl, combine buttermilk, margarine, egg, and vanilla. Pour this mixture into the dry ingredients (made in step #3).

5. Using a large spoon, gently stir ingredients just until moist (do not over-mix). Add fruit and stir gently (do not over-mix).

6. Spoon batter evenly into 9 muffin cups.

7. Bake 20 to 25 minutes or until golden brown.

8. Serve hot or cold. Muffins may be frozen for later use.

Per serving: 130 calories, 3.5 g fat, 3 g protein, 22 g carbohydrate, 25 mg cholesterol, 105 mg sodium

Cost: Per Recipe: $ 1.51; Per Serving: $ 0.17

Desserts

Apple Crisp

Serving Size: 1/8 of recipe
Yield: 8 servings

Ingredients:

4-5 medium apples
1/4 cup quick-cooking oatmeal
1/4 cup flour
1/2 cup brown sugar
1 Tablespoon cinnamon
1/4 cup margarine

Instructions:

1. Preheat the oven to 350 degrees.

2. Grease the bottom and sides of the square pan.

3. Remove the cores from the apples. Slice the apples.

4. Spread the sliced apples on the bottom of the pan.

5. Cut the margarine into small pieces and put in a medium-sized bowl.

6. Add the oatmeal, flour, brown sugar and cinnamon.

7. Using two knives, cut the margarine into the mixture until it looks like small crumbs.

8. Sprinkle the mixture over the top of the apples.

9. Bake in the oven for about 20 minutes.

Note: For different tastes, try other fruits like cherries, pears, peaches, or plums.

Per serving: 160 calories, 6 g fat, 1 g protein, 28 g carbohydrate, 0 mg cholesterol, 50 mg sodium

Cost: Per Recipe: $ 2.10; Per Serving: $ 0.26

Applesauce Cookies

Serving Size: 2 cookies
Yield: 12 servings

Ingredients:

1 cup sugar
1/2 cup margarine or butter or shortening
1 egg
2 teaspoons baking soda
2 1/2 cup all purpose flour
1/2 teaspoon salt
1 teaspoon cinnamon
1 1/2 cup applesauce, unsweetened
1 cup raisins
1 cup nuts (optional)

Instructions:

1. Preheat oven to 350°F. Lightly oil or spray a baking sheet with cooking spray.

2. Cream together sugar, shortening and egg.

3. In a separate bowl, combine baking soda, flour, salt, and cinnamon. Mix well.

4. Stir flour mixture into shortening mixture just until moist.

5. Add applesauce, raisins, and nuts.

6. Drop dough by heaping teaspoon several inches apart on a greased baking sheet. Bake for 10 to 12 minutes.

Per serving: 290 calories, 8 g fat, 4 g protein, 51 g carbohydrate, 20 mg cholesterol, 380 mg sodium

Cost: Per Recipe: $ 2.28; Per Serving: $ 0.19

Applesauce Loaf Cake

Serving Size: 1/16 of recipe
Yield: 16 servings

Ingredients:

1/2 cup chopped walnuts
1 1/2 cups applesauce
1 egg
1 cup sugar
2 Tablespoons oil
1 teaspoon vanilla extract
2 cups all purpose flour
2 teaspoons baking soda
1/2 teaspoon ground cinnamon
1/2 teaspoon ground nutmeg
1 cup raisins

Instructions:

1. Preheat the oven to 350 degrees. Grease 2 (8x4x2 inch) loaf pans.

2. Toast walnuts in an ungreased skillet pan. Stir while heating on medium-low heat for 5-7 minutes. They are done when they are brown and smell nutty. Set aside to cool.

3. Mix applesauce, egg, sugar, oil and vanilla in a large bowl.

4. Mix flour, baking soda, cinnamon, and nutmeg together in a smaller bowl.

5. Pour flour mixture into applesauce mixture.

6. Stir in raisins and cooled toasted nuts.

7. Pour half of the batter into each greased pan. Bake for 45-55 minutes.

8. Remove cakes from the oven. Cool for 10 minutes. Remove from pans to finish cooling. For best taste, let cakes cool a few hours before serving.

Per serving: 200 calories, 4.5 g fat, 3 g protein, 38 g carbohydrate, 10 mg cholesterol, 170 mg sodium

Cost: Per Recipe: $ 2.56; Per Serving: $ 0.16

Cran-Apple Crisp

Serving Size: 3/4 cup
Yield: 8 servings

Ingredients:

4 cored and thinly sliced apples
1 can (16 ounce) whole cranb

erry sauce
2 teaspoon soft melted margarine
1 cup uncooked oatmeal
1/3 cup brown sugar
1 teaspoon cinnamon

Instructions:

1. Preheat oven to 400 degrees.

2. Wash apples, remove cores and slice thinly, keeping peel on.

3. In a bowl, combine the cranberries and apples. Pour into an 8x8 inch pan.

4. Combine melted margarine with oatmeal, brown sugar, and cinnamon until well blended. Sprinkle over apple/cranberry mixture.

5. Cover and bake for 15 minutes.

6. Uncover and bake 10 more minutes until the topping is crisp and brown.

7. Serve warm or cold.

Per serving: 220 calories, 2 g fat, 2 g protein, 52 g carbohydrate, 0 mg cholesterol, 25 mg sodium

Cost: Per Recipe: $ 2.91; Per Serving: $ 0.36

Banana Waldorf

Serving Size: 1/4 of recipe
Yield: 4 servings

Ingredients:

3 bananas - peeled and sliced
1 apple - cored and sliced, with peel
4 cups nonfat vanilla yogurt
1 pinch cinnamon
2 Tablespoons ground walnuts

Instructions:

1. Mix all ingredients together in large mixing bowl.

2. Place in individual serving dishes and chill until ready to serve, up to 1 hour.

3. This dessert looks great when topped with a sprinkle of ground cinnamon.

Per serving: 240 calories, 2 g fat, 9 g protein, 48 g carbohydrate, 5 mg cholesterol, 140 mg sodium

Cost: Per Recipe: $ 3.34; Per Serving: $ 0.83

Bananas with Caramel Sauce

Serving Size: 1/2 banana
Yield: 12 servings

Ingredients:

6 large bananas
6 Tablespoons butter
3 teaspoons water
1 cup sugar
1/2 cup evaporated milk, skim
2 teaspoons cornstarch, dissolved in 2 teaspoons water

Instructions:

1. Preheat oven to 400 degrees. Place unpeeled bananas on a baking sheet. Prick the skin of each banana several times with the prongs of a fork. Cook the bananas for about 8 minutes. The skin will turn black.

2. Over moderate heat, cook the butter, water and sugar to a medium brown color (it will look like caramel). Remove from heat.

3. Combine the milk, cornstarch slurry to the caramel mixture. Stir to dissolve.

4. Return to the heat and bring to a boil, stirring constantly.

5. Remove from heat and cool slightly.

6. Serve on top of the bananas that have been peeled and sliced lengthwise.

Per serving: 190 calories, 6 g fat, 2 g protein, 34 g carbohydrate, 15 mg cholesterol, 15 mg sodium

Cost: Per Recipe: $ 1.76; Per Serving: $ 0.15

Banana and Pudding Dessert

Serving Size: 1/8 of recipe
Yield: 8 servings

Ingredients:

1 box (3.5 ounce) instant pudding mix, banana or vanilla flavor
2 cups non-fat or low-fat (1%) milk
8 ounces yogurt, fat free or non-dairy whipped topping
2 sliced bananas or other sliced fruit

Instructions:

1. In a medium bowl, combine milk and pudding. Beat with wooden spoon, wire whisk, or electric mixer on lowest speed for 2 minutes

2. Gently mix yogurt (or whipped topping) with pudding mixture. Refrigerate for 30 minutes.

3. Layer fruit slices in the bottom of 8 dessert cups.

4. Pour the pudding mixture over sliced fruit.

5. Refrigerate until ready to serve, at least 5 minutes, though it's better if it's refrigerated longer.

Per serving: 110 calories, 0 g fat, 4 g protein, 24 g carbohydrate, 0 mg cholesterol, 230 mg sodium

Cost: Per Recipe: $ 1.88; Per Serving: $ 0.24

Blueberry Coffee Cake

Serving Size: 1/8 of recipe
Yield: 8 servings

Ingredients:

1 egg
1/2 cup nonfat milk
1/2 cup yogurt, nonfat vanilla
3 Tablespoons canola oil
2 teaspoons grated lemon peel (yellow only)
2 cups flour
1/2 cup sugar
4 teaspoons baking powder
1/2 teaspoon salt
1 1/2 cup fresh (or frozen unsweetened) blueberries

For the topping:
3 Tablespoons sugar
2 Tablespoons coarsely chopped walnuts
1/4 teaspoon cinnamon

Instructions:

1. Position rack in the center of the oven. Preheat oven to 400 degrees.

2. In a large bowl whisk together the egg, milk, yogurt, oil and lemon peel.

3. Sift the flour, sugar, baking powder and salt onto the liquid ingredients. Using a fork, stir very lightly, just until ingredients are combined.

4. Gently fold in the blueberries. Pour the batter into an 8- or 9-inch baking pan coated with nonstick spray.

5. In a small bowl combine the topping ingredients. Sprinkle evenly over the cake batter.

6. Bake at 400 degrees for 30 to 35 minutes or until the top is lightly browned and a wooden toothpick inserted in the center comes out clean.

7. Allow the cake to cool in the baking pan on a wire rack for at least 10 minutes.

8. Serve warm or at room temperature.

Note: When tightly wrapped in plastic wrap, this coffee cake will keep for 3 to 4 days in the refrigerator. It also freezes very well.

Per serving: 250 calories, 6 g fat, 6 g protein, 45 g carbohydrate, 25 mg cholesterol, 420 mg sodium

Cost: Per Recipe: $ 2.34; Per Serving: $ 0.29

Carrot Cookies

Serving Size: 2 cookies
Yield: 30 servings

Ingredients:

1/2 cup soft margarine
1 cup honey*
1 cup grated raw carrots
2 well beaten egg whites
2 cups all purpose flour
2 teaspoons baking powder
1/4 teaspoon baking soda
1/4 teaspoon salt
1 teaspoon cinnamon
2 cups raw oatmeal, quick cooking
1 cup raisins

Instructions:

1. Preheat oven to 350 degrees.

2. In a large bowl, cream together margarine and honey. Stir in carrots and egg whites.

3. Stir together flour, baking powder, baking soda, salt, cinnamon, oatmeal and raisins. Gradually stir flour-oatmeal mixture into creamed mixture, just until all flour is mixed. Do not over mix.

4. Drop from teaspoon on greased baking sheet. Flatten slightly and bake for 10 minutes, or until lightly browned.

*Note: Instead of honey, you can use 1 1/4 cups sugar mixed with 1/4 cup water.

Per serving: 130 calories, 3.5 g fat, 2 g protein, 24 g carbohydrate, 0 mg cholesterol, 100 mg sodium

Cost: Per Recipe: $ 3.09; Per Serving: $ 0.10

Chocolate Mousse

Serving Size: 1/4 of recipe
Yield: 4 servings

Ingredients:

1 small box instant chocolate pudding mix
1 1/4 cup cold soy milk
1 package (10.5 ounce) silken tofu

Instructions:

1. Blend the chocolate pudding mix and the soy milk on medium speed for about 15 seconds until the mixture is very smooth.

2. Add the silken tofu and blend again. Scrape the mixture down off the sides to be sure it's all mixed in. Blend and scrape until well mixed and very smooth.

3. Pour mixture into 4 small serving dishes.

4. Place in the fridge. Chill for at least 2 hours before serving.

Per serving: 170 calories, 4 g fat, 8 g protein, 28 g carbohydrate, 0 mg cholesterol, 400 mg sodium

Cost: Per Recipe: $ 2.53; Per Serving: $ 0.63

Custard

Serving Size: 1/2 cup
Yield: 4 servings

Ingredients:

1 egg*
2 Tablespoons sugar
1 cup skim milk or reconstituted non-fat dry milk
1/4 to 1/2 teaspoon vanilla (optional)

Instructions:

Stovetop version:

1. Beat egg and sugar together in a saucepan.

2. Add milk.

3. Place saucepan with egg/milk mixture in another pan containing 1-2 inches boiling water.

4. Stir custard constantly while cooking. Cook until foam disappears and custard coats the spoon. Remove from heat.

5. Add flavoring and stir. Pour into individual dishes and cool in the refrigerator. Custard will be soft.

Baked version:

1. Beat together egg and sugar in a baking dish.

2. Add milk and flavorings. Mix thoroughly.

3. Set baking dish in a shallow pan of hot water.

4. Bake at 350 degrees until the tip of a knife inserted in the center of the custard comes out clean (50-60 minutes). Do not overcook. Eat warm or refrigerate for later.

***Note:** In both versions, an additional egg can be added during step 1.

Per serving: 70 calories, 1 g fat, 4 g protein, 10 g carbohydrate, 55 mg cholesterol, 50 mg sodium

Cost: Per Recipe: $ 0.37; Per Serving: $ 0.09

Bread Pudding with Vanilla Sauce

Serving Size: 1/6 of recipe
Yield: 6 servings

Ingredients:

1 Tablespoon margarine
5 slices whole wheat bread
3 eggs
1/3 cup sugar
pinch of salt
2 cups nonfat milk
1 teaspoon vanilla
1/4 cup raisins
1 teaspoon cinnamon and/or nutmeg

For Vanilla Sauce:
1 Tablespoon cornstarch
1/3 cup sugar
water
1 Tablespoon margarine or butter
1 1/2 teaspoon vanilla extract

Instructions:

1. Melt margarine in medium size skillet.

2. Tear bread in pieces and spread on bottom of skillet.

3. Beat eggs and stir in sugar, salt, warmed milk and vanilla. Sprinkle raisins over bread and pour egg mixture over all.

4. Cover and cook over very low heat for 20 minutes.

5. Pudding is done when custard is set in the middle.

6. Allow to cool in the skillet.

7. Prepare vanilla sauce while pudding cools.

8. Combine cornstarch and sugar in a small saucepan. Gradually add water, stirring well.

9. Cook until thick and clear, stirring constantly.

10. Add margarine and vanilla, stirring until margarine melts.

11. Spoon over individual servings of bread pudding.

Per serving: 270 calories, 7 g fat, 9 g protein, 45 g carbohydrate, 105 mg cholesterol, 250 mg sodium

Cost: Per Recipe: $ 1.95; Per Serving: $ 0.33

Rice Pudding

Serving Size: 1/4 cup
Yield: 8 servings

Ingredients:

1 cup milk, whole
1 cup water
1 cup rice, uncooked
2 large eggs
1 cup milk, evaporated
1 teaspoon vanilla
1/4 cup sugar
1/8 teaspoon ground cinnamon

Instructions:

1. In a saucepan, heat milk and water.

2. Add rice, bring to a boil, lower heat to simmer; stir mixture every 10 minutes. Cook uncovered until rice is tender, about 30 minutes.

3. In a large bowl, mix eggs, 3/4 cup evaporated milk, vanilla, and sugar. Set aside.

4. Add remaining 1/4 cup evaporated milk to rice mixture.

5. Spoon 1 cup of rice mixture into egg mixture and stir. Pour egg-rice mixture into remaining rice.

6. Heat pudding until it boils, stirring continuously. Remove from heat, and sprinkle with cinnamon.

Per serving: 190 calories, 4.5 g fat, 6 g protein, 29 g carbohydrate, 65 mg cholesterol, 60 mg sodium

Cost: Per Recipe: $ 1.40; Per Serving: $ 0.18

Cornmeal Pudding

Serving Size: 1 square
Yield: 8 servings

Ingredients:

2 1/2 cups nonfat milk
1/2 cup cornmeal
1/2 cup cold nonfat milk
1 Tablespoon margarine
1/4 - 1/2 cup molasses
1/2 teaspoon ginger
1/2 teaspoon cinnamon

Instructions:

1. Preheat oven to 325 degrees. Lightly grease 1-quart baking pan.

2. In a saucepan, heat 2 1/2 cups of milk to a simmer.

3. In a bowl, mix together the other 1/2 cup cold milk with cornmeal.

4. Add cornmeal mixture to warm milk, stir well.

5. Cook 20 minutes over low-medium heat. Stir often to prevent scorching. Cook until thickened.

6. Remove pudding from heat. Stir in margarine, molasses, ginger and cinnamon.

7. Pour into the greased baking pan.

8. Bake for 55 to 60 minutes. When a knife is inserted and comes out clean, the pudding is done.

9. Cut into 8 squares before serving. Serve warm.

Per serving: 110 calories, 1.5 g fat, 4 g protein, 19 g carbohydrate, 0 mg cholesterol, 65 mg sodium

Cost: Per Recipe: $ 1.68; Per Serving: $ 0.21

Fruit Pizza

Serving Size: 1/12 of recipe
Yield: 12 servings

Ingredients:

Cookie Crust:
1/2 cup margarine
1/2 cup sugar
1 teaspoon vanilla extract
1 large egg
2 cups flour
2 teaspoons baking powder

Cheese Spread:
8 ounces cream cheese, non-fat or light
1/2 cup sugar
1 teaspoon vanilla extract

Fruit Topping Ideas:
1 cup sliced strawberries or kiwi, bananas, pears, peaches, or blueberries

Instructions:

1. Preheat oven to 375 degrees.

2. For crust, cream margarine, sugar vanilla, and egg until light and fluffy. Add flour and baking powder, mixing well.

3. Spread mixture about 1/8 inch thick on a pizza pan, baking sheet, or 9 inch by 13 inch pan.

4. Bake for 10 to 12 minutes or until lightly browned. Cool.

5. For spread, mix together cream cheese, sugar, and vanilla. Spread on cooled cookie crust.

6. Arrange fruit on top of pizza. Refrigerate until serving time.

Per serving: 240 calories, 8 g fat, 6 g protein, 35 g carbohydrate, 15 mg cholesterol, 280 mg sodium

Cost: Per Recipe: $ 2.33; Per Serving: $ 0.19

Fresh Fruit with Cinnamon Yogurt Dip

Serving Size: 1/4 of recipe
Yield: 4 servings

Ingredients:

1 apple
1 orange
1/4 cup orange juice
1 cup vanilla yogurt
1/2 teaspoon cinnamon

Instructions:

1. Core and slice the apple.

2. Slice banana into thin circles.

3. Peel the orange and break it into sections.

4. Pour the orange juice into a small bowl.

5. Dip the fruit pieces into the orange juice to prevent browning.

6. Arrange on a plate.

7. Mix the yogurt and cinnamon in a small bowl.

8. Put the bowl of yogurt and cinnamon next to the fruit. Use it as a dip for the fruit.

Note: Try making this with other favorite fruits.

Per serving: 120 calories, 1 g fat, 4 g protein, 25 g carbohydrate, 5 mg cholesterol, 40 mg sodium

Cost: Per Recipe: $ 1.54; Per Serving: $ 0.39

Pocket Fruit Pies

Serving Size: 1 pie
Yield: 4 servings

Ingredients:

4 (8 inch) flour tortillas
2 medium peaches, pears, or apples
1/4 teaspoon ground cinnamon
2 Tablespoons brown sugar
1/8 teaspoon ground nutmeg
2 Tablespoons milk
sugar (optional)

Instructions:

1. Warm tortillas in microwave or oven to make them easier to handle.

2. Peel and chop fruit into pieces.

3. Place 1/4 of the fruit on half of each tortilla.

4. In a small bowl, stir together brown sugar, cinnamon and nutmeg. Sprinkle over fruit.

5. Roll up the tortillas, starting at the end with the fruit.

6. Place on an un-greased baking sheet and make small slashes to allow steam to escape. Brush with milk and sprinkle with additional sugar, if desired.

7. Back at 350 degree in oven for 8-12 minutes or until lightly brown.

8. Serve warm or cool.

 Safety Tip: Allow pie to cool slightly before tasting - the steam and sugar can burn.

Per serving: 210 calories, 4 g fat, 4 g protein, 40 g carbohydrate, 0 mg cholesterol, 320 mg sodium

Cost: Per Recipe: $ 1.27; Per Serving: $ 0.32

Honey Milk Balls

Serving Size: 2 honey milk balls
Yield: 20 servings

Ingredients:

1/4 cup honey
1/4 cup peanut butter
1/2 cup dry milk, nonfat
1/2 cup crushed cereal

Instructions:

1. Mix honey and peanut butter.

2. Gradually add dry milk and mix well.

3. Chill for easier handling.

4. With greased hands, form into small balls.

5. Roll in crushed cereal flakes.

6. Chill until firm.

Safety tip: Honey should not be given to children less than one year of age.

Per serving: 40 calories, 1.5 g fat, 1 g protein, 6 g carbohydrate, 0 mg cholesterol, 15 mg sodium

Cost: Per Recipe: $ 1.37; Per Serving: $ 0.07

Peach Cobbler

Serving Size: 1/4 of recipe
Yield: 4 servings

Ingredients:

1 can (16 ounce) sliced peaches, packed in juice
1 egg
1/3 cup sugar
1/2 cup flour
1/2 teaspoon baking powder
1/4 teaspoon salt
1 Tablespoon softened margarine

Instructions:

1. Preheat the oven to 375 degrees.

2. Open the can of peaches. Pour the peaches and their juice into the casserole dish. Heat them on the stove-top until they bubble.

3. Slightly beat 1 egg.

4. In a mixing bowl, mix the egg, sugar, flour, baking powder, salt, and margarine.

5. Drop spoonfuls of this mixture on top of the hot, bubbling peaches.

6. Use pot holders to carefully remove the casserole dish from the stove.

7. Put the casserole dish in the oven. Bake for about 30-40 minutes.

Per serving: 210 calories, 4 g fat, 4 g protein, 42 g carbohydrate, 55 mg cholesterol, 250 mg sodium

Cost: Per Recipe: $ 1.27; Per Serving: $ 0.32

Peach Crisp

Serving Size: 1/6 of recipe
Yield: 6 servings

Ingredients:

4 peaches (4 cups sliced)
2 Tablespoons margarine
3/4 cup quick-cooking oats
1/2 cup sugar
1/4 cup flour
2 teaspoons cinnamon
1 teaspoon lemon juice

Instructions:

1. Preheat the oven to 375 degrees.

2. Wash and slice the peaches.

3. Spread the peach slices on the bottom of the baking pan.

4. Melt the margarine in a saucepan.

5. In a small bowl, mix everything but the peaches. Stir until the mix is well blended.

6. Sprinkle the oat mix on top of the peaches.

7. Bake for 20 minutes.

Notes: Serve the peach crisp either hot or cold. To remove the peach fuzz, you can rub the washed peach gently with a paper towel.

Per serving: 200 calories, 4.5 g fat, 3 g protein, 40 g carbohydrate, 0 mg cholesterol, 30 mg sodium

Cost: Per Recipe: $ 1.62; Per Serving: $ 0.27

Pineapple Rice Bake

Serving Size: 1/6 of recipe
Yield: 6 servings

Ingredients:

4 eggs
1 cup milk
1/2 cup sugar
1 can (8 ounce) pineapple, crushed, undrained
1/2 teaspoon cinnamon (optional)
1/2 teaspoon nutmeg (optional)
1 teaspoon vanilla
3 cups cooked rice

Instructions:

1. Preheat oven to 350 degrees. Lightly coat an oven-safe 2 quart casserole dish with nonstick spray or oil.

2. In a large mixing bowl, beat together eggs, milk and sugar.

3. Add undrained crushed pineapple, cinnamon, nutmeg and vanilla.

4. Stir in cooked rice. Pour into prepared casserole dish.

5. Bake for 50 to 60 minutes or until a knife inserted in center of pudding comes out clean.

Per serving: 260 calories, 4 g fat, 8 g protein, 47 g carbohydrate, 145 mg cholesterol, 70 mg sodium

Cost: Per Recipe: $ 1.65; Per Serving: $ 0.27

Pineapple Zucchini Cake

Serving Size: 1/12 of recipe
Yield: 12 servings

Ingredients:

3 eggs
2 cups sugar
2 teaspoons vanilla
1 cup vegetable oil
2 cups peeled, grated zucchini
1 teaspoon baking powder
1 teaspoon salt
1 teaspoon baking soda
3 cups all purpose flour
1 cup pineapple, crushed, drained
1/2 cup raisins (optional)
1 cup chopped pecans (optional)

Instructions:

1. Preheat oven to 350 degrees. Grease or lightly spray with non-stick cooking spray, a 9 x 13 inch pan.

2. In a large bowl, beat eggs, sugar, vanilla, and oil. Add zucchini.

3. In a separate bowl, combine baking powder salt, baking soda and flour. Add dry ingredients to creamed mixture.

4. Stir in fruit and nuts.

5. Bake for 45 to 50 minutes, or until cake springs back when lightly pressed with your finger.

Note: Try adding 1/2 cup shredded coconut for added flavor.

Per serving: 440 calories, 20 g fat, 5 g protein, 61 g carbohydrate, 55 mg cholesterol, 360 mg sodium

Cost: Per Recipe: $ 2.87; Per Serving: $ 0.24

Pumpkin Cake

Serving Size: 2 squares
Yield: 30 servings

Ingredients:

1/3 cup dry milk, nonfat
2 cups all purpose flour
1 teaspoon baking soda
2 1/2 teaspoons cinnamon
1/2 teaspoon cloves
1/2 teaspoon allspice
1/2 teaspoon nutmeg
1/3 cup vegetable oil
2/3 cup honey
1/2 cup orange juice
2 Tablespoons grated orange peel
2 eggs
1 cup mashed pumpkin

Instructions:

1. Preheat oven to 350 degrees. Lightly grease or spray with nonstick spray a 12 x 15 inch baking pan with sides.

2. In a small bowl, combine dry milk, flour, baking soda, and spices. Set aside.

3. In a large bowl, thoroughly mix oil, honey, juice, peel, eggs and pumpkin.

4. Gradually add flour mixture to pumpkin mixture, stirring until smooth.

5. Spread batter onto prepared baking pan. Bake for 15 to 20 minutes, or until golden brown and cake springs back when lightly touched with your finger. Cool. Cut into squares.

Per serving: 90 calories, 3 g fat, 2 g protein, 14 g carbohydrate, 15 mg cholesterol, 50 mg sodium

Cost: Per Recipe: $ 4.74; Per Serving: $ 0.16

Pumpkin Cheese Pie

Serving Size: 1 slice
Yield: 16 servings

Ingredients:

8 ounces cream cheese, reduced fat
8 ounces cream cheese, nonfat
2 eggs
4 egg whites
1 1/4 cups sugar
1 can (29 ounces) pumpkin
1 teaspoon ginger
1 Tablespoon cinnamon
2 - 9 inch graham cracker pie crusts

Instructions:

1. Preheat oven to 350 degrees.

2. Place the cream cheese, eggs, and sugar in a large mixing bowl. Mix at medium speed until creamed. Add the remaining ingredients and mix at medium speed until ingredients are well mixed.

3. Spoon the mixture evenly in each pie crust and place both in the oven for approximately 50 minutes until pies look firm in the middle.

Per serving: 290 calories, 11 g fat, 7 g protein, 42 g carbohydrate, 35 mg cholesterol, 310 mg sodium

Cost: Per Recipe: $ 10.05; Per Serving: $ 0.63

Wobbly Wonders

Serving Size: 1/20 of recipe
Yield: 20 servings

Ingredients:

12 ounces flavored gelatin - choose your favorite
2 cups boiling water
1 1/2 cups low-fat milk
1 package (3 1/2 ounce) instant vanilla pudding

Instructions:

1. In a medium bowl, dissolve gelatin in boiling water. Cool at least 30 minutes.

2. Pour milk into large mixing bowl and add pudding mix. Using an electric mixer, beat 1 minute.

3. Gradually add and beat in gelatin mixture. Pour into a 9x13 inch baking pan. Chill in fridge for several hours.

4. Cut fun shapes with cookie cutters or knife. Store in refrigerator.

Per serving: 90 calories, 0 g fat, 2 g protein, 20 g carbohydrate, 0 mg cholesterol, 150 mg sodium

Cost: Per Recipe: $ 2.41; Per Serving: $ 0.12

sauces, CONDIMENTS & DreSSINGS

Turkey Gravy

Serving Size: 1/6 of recipe
Yield: 6 servings

Ingredients:

2 Tablespoons margarine or butter or turkey drippings
3 Tablespoons flour
1/4 teaspoon salt
1 1/2 cups chicken or turkey broth
1/2 cup cooked and chopped giblets

Instructions:

1. Melt margarine in skillet over low heat. Mix in flour and salt. Stir and heat until bubbly.

2. Add broth slowly, stirring constantly. Cook over low heat for 5- 10 minutes.

3. Add the cooked giblets. Heat a few minutes to blend flavors.

Per serving: 70 calories, 4.5 g fat, 4 g protein, 3 g carbohydrate, 55 mg cholesterol, 370 mg sodium

Cost: Per Recipe: $ 0.93; Per Serving: $ 0.15

White Sauce – Thin

Serving Size: variable
Yield: 1 serving

Ingredients:

1 Tablespoon butter
1 Tablespoon flour
salt and pepper to taste
1 cup liquid milk, nonfat or 1/3 cup powdered milk and
water to equal 1 cup

Instructions:

1. In a small pot, melt butter over low heat.

2. Add flour, salt, and pepper to mixture.

3. Add milk gradually.

4. Heat to boiling, stir constantly until mixture is smooth
and bubbly. (The consistency should be like thin cream.)

5. Remove from heat.

Note: Use for cream soups and stews.

Per recipe: 220 calories, 11 g fat, 10 g protein, 19 g
carbohydrate, 35 mg cholesterol, 210 mg sodium

Cost: Per Recipe: $ 0.27; Per Serving: $ 0.27

Asian Salad Dressing

Serving Size: 2 Tablespoons
Yield: 5 servings

Ingredients:

2 Tablespoons vegetable oil
3 Tablespoons red vinegar
2 water
2 teaspoons low-sodium soy sauce
2 Tablespoons brown sugar
2 Tablespoons lemon juice
1/2 teaspoon garlic powder

Instructions:

1. Put all the ingredients in a jar or bottle with a lid.

2. Put on the lid. Shake well.

3. Chill in the fridge for at least 1 hour before serving.

Notes: Try this dressing on cut vegetables or salad. After serving, keep any leftover dressing in the refrigerator.

Per serving: 70 calories, 6 g fat, 0 g protein, 6 g carbohydrate, 0 mg cholesterol, 75 mg sodium

Cost: Per Recipe: $ 0.29; Per Serving: $ 0.06

Creamy Dill Dip & Dressing

Serving Size: 2 Tablespoons
Yield: 16 servings

Ingredients:

1 cup sour cream, nonfat
1 cup yogurt, nonfat plain
2 Tablespoons dried dill

Instructions:

1. Put the sour cream, yogurt, and dill in a medium bowl. Stir together.

2. Store the dip in a covered container if you don't plan to eat it right away.

3. Keep the dip in the refrigerator until you serve it.

Notes: Serve with cucumber slices. If you want a creamy salad dressing, add a few tablespoons of water to the dip.

Per serving of dip: 20 calories, 0 g fat, 1 g protein, 4 g carbohydrate, 5 mg cholesterol, 30 mg sodium

Cost: Per Recipe: $ 3.27; Per Serving: $ 0.20

French Dressing

Serving Size: 2 Tablespoons
Yield: 5 servings

Ingredients:

2 Tablespoons vegetable oil
1/4 cup ketchup
1 teaspoon sugar
1 Tablespoon vinegar
1/2 teaspoon paprika
1 Tablespoon grated onion
1 Tablespoon lemon juice

Instructions:

1. Put all the ingredients in a jar or bottle with a lid.

2. Put on the lid. Shake well.

3. Chill in the fridge for at least 1 hour before serving.

Notes: Try this dressing on cut vegetables or salad. After serving, keep any leftover dressing in the refrigerator.

Per serving: 70 calories, 6 g fat, 0 g protein, 4 g carbohydrate, 0 mg cholesterol, 135 mg sodium

Cost: Per Recipe: $ 0.41; Per Serving: $ 0.08

Honey Mustard Dressing

Serving Size: 2 Tablespoons
Yield: 7 servings

Ingredients:

1/4 cup vegetable oil
1/4 cup vinegar
2 Tablespoons honey
2 Tablespoons mustard
2 teaspoons lemon juice
1/4 teaspoon black pepper

Instructions:

1. Put all the ingredients in a jar or bottle with a lid.

2. Put on the lid. Shake well.

3. Chill in the fridge for at least 1 hour before serving.

Notes: Try this dressing on cold cooked pasta and vegetables. After serving, keep any leftover dressing in the refrigerator.

Per serving: 90 calories, 8 g fat, 0 g protein, 5 g carbohydrate, 0 mg cholesterol, 50 mg sodium

Cost: Per Recipe: $ 1.16; Per Serving: $ 0.17

Italian Dressing

Serving Size: 2 Tablespoons
Yield: 8 servings

Ingredients:

1/2 teaspoon garlic powder or 1 fresh clove, minced
1 teaspoon Italian herb mix
1 Tablespoon Parmesan cheese
1/4 teaspoon ground black pepper
1/2 teaspoon celery salt
1/2 cup vinegar
1/4 cup vegetable oil
1/2 cup water

Instructions:

1. Combine all ingredients in a pint-sized jar with tight fitting lid.

2. Shake vigorously to blend ingredients.

3. Store refrigerated.

Per serving: 70 calories, 7 g fat, 0 g protein, 0 g carbohydrate, 0 mg cholesterol, 80 mg sodium

Cost: Per Recipe: $ 1.19; Per Serving: $ 0.15

Sweet and Sour Dressing

Serving Size: 2 Tablespoons
Yield: 4 servings

Ingredients:

1/2 cup sugar
1 Tablespoon cornstarch
1/2 cup vinegar

Instructions:

1. In a small saucepan, combine sugar and cornstarch.

2. Stir in vinegar.

3. Cook over medium heat until slightly thickened and clear.

4. Chill before serving. Store refrigerated.

Per serving: 110 calories, 0 g fat, 0 g protein, 27 g carbohydrate, 0 mg cholesterol, 0 mg sodium

Cost: Per Recipe: $ 1.03; Per Serving: $ 0.26

Thousand Island Dressing

Serving Size: 2 Tablespoons
Yield: 8 servings

Ingredients:

1/2 cup yogurt, nonfat plain
1/2 cup mayonnaise, reduced-fat
1/4 cup chili sauce
2 Tablespoons sweet pickle relish
1 Tablespoon finely chopped onion
1 Tablespoon finely chopped celery
1 teaspoon lemon (or lime) juice
1/8 teaspoon black pepper

Instructions:

1. Mix ingredients together.

2. Chill and serve over vegetables or on a salad.

3. Store refrigerated.

Per serving: 70 calories, 5 g fat, 1 g protein, 7 g carbohydrate, 5 mg cholesterol, 380 mg sodium

Cost: Per Recipe: $ 1.18; Per Serving: $ 0.15

Bean Dip

Serving Size: 1/2 cup
Yield: 6 servings

Ingredients:

2 cups canned kidney beans
1 Tablespoon vinegar
3/4 teaspoon chili powder
1/8 teaspoon ground cumin
2 teaspoons finely chopped onion
1 cup grated cheddar cheese

Instructions:

1. Drain the kidney beans, but save the liquid in a small bowl

2. Place the beans, vinegar, chili powder and cumin in a blender. Blend until smooth. Add enough saved bean liquid to make the dip easy to spread.

3. Stir in the chopped onion and grated cheese.

4. Store in a tightly covered container and place in the fridge

5. Serve with raw vegetable sticks or crackers.

Notes: If you don't have a blender, you can mix the first 4 ingredients in a medium bowl and mash with a fork. Then stir in the onion and cheese.

You can store this dip in the refrigerator for up to 4 or 5 days.

Per serving: 150 calories, 7 g fat, 9 g protein, 14 g carbohydrate, 20 mg cholesterol, 410 mg sodium

Cost: Per Recipe: $ 2.15; Per Serving: $ 0.36

Eggplant and Pepper Dip

Serving Size: 1/4 cup
Yield: 8 servings

Ingredients:

1 large eggplant
2 red peppers
1 small onion
1/4 teaspoon garlic powder
2 Tablespoons vegetable oil
1 teaspoon oregano
1 teaspoon basil
1/4 teaspoon salt

Instructions:

1. Preheat oven to 400 degrees.

2. Use a vegetable peeler to remove the peel from the eggplant.

3. Chop the eggplant into 1 inch cubes.

4. Chop the red peppers.

5. Peel and chop the onion.

6. Put all the ingredients in a large bowl. Stir together.

7. Spread the ingredients on a baking tray.

8. Bake for 45 minutes. While the dip is baking, stir it a few times.

9. When the eggplant is lightly browned and soft, take the dip out of the oven.

10. Let the dip cool for at least 10 minutes.

11. Put the dip the blender. Blend until smooth.

12. Serve the dip cold or at room temperature.

Notes: Try this low-fat dip with cut vegetables, toast, or as a spread on sandwiches.

Per serving: 60 calories, 3.5 g fat, 1 g protein, 6 g carbohydrate, 0 mg cholesterol, 75 mg sodium

Cost: Per Recipe: $ 3.21; Per Serving: $ 0.40

Creamy Peanut Dip

Serving Size: 2 Tablespoons
Yield: 6 servings

Ingredients:

1/4 cup creamy peanut butter
2 Tablespoons orange juice
1/2 cup yogurt, low-fat vanilla

Instructions:

1. In a small bowl, mix the peanut butter and orange juice until smooth.

2. Stir in the vanilla yogurt.

3. Cover and put in the refrigerator until chilled.

Note: Serve with fresh apples, pears, carrot sticks or celery sticks.

Per serving: 80 calories, 5 g fat, 4 g protein, 6 g carbohydrate, 0 mg cholesterol, 15 mg sodium

Cost: Per Recipe: $ 0.74; Per Serving: $ 0.12

Herbed Dip

Serving Size: 2 Tablespoons
Yield: 10 servings

Ingredients:

1 cup cottage cheese, low-fat
4 Tablespoons yogurt, low-fat plain
1 Tablespoons chopped onion or chives
1 teaspoon dried parsley
1/4 teaspoon dried dill

Instructions:

1. Place all the ingredients in a blender.

2. Blend all the ingredients thoroughly.

3. Pour the mixture into a clean container.

4. Cover and chill.

Note: Serve on crackers, or as dip for fresh raw
vegetables.

Per serving: 20 calories, 0 g fat, 3 g protein, 1 g
carbohydrate, 0 mg cholesterol, 95 mg sodium

Cost: Per Recipe: $ 1.32; Per Serving: $ 0.13

Ranch Dip

Serving Size: 1/2 cup
Yield: 4 servings

Ingredients:

1 can (15 ounce) great northern beans, rinsed and drained
1/4 cup water
1/2 cup yogurt, plain low-fat
1/2 teaspoon garlic powder
1/8 teaspoon cayenne pepper
1/4 teaspoon black pepper
1 Tablespoon chopped fresh chives
1 Tablespoon chopped fresh parsley
1/4 teaspoon dried tarragon
1/4 teaspoon salt
1 Tablespoon lemon juice

Instructions:

1. Blend the beans and garlic in a blender, adding enough water for the desired consistency.

2. Blend for 2 minutes to make it silky smooth.

3. Use a spatula to scrape the mixture into a medium bowl.

4. Stir in the yogurt, cayenne, chives, parsley, and tarragon, salt and lemon juice. Serve in a bowl.

Per serving: 150 calories, 1 g fat, 10 g protein, 26 g carbohydrate, 0 mg cholesterol, 170 mg sodium

Cost: Per Recipe: $ 1.06; Per Serving: $ 0.27

South of the Border Dip

Serving Size: 2 Tablespoons
Yield: 16 servings

Ingredients:

1 cup sour cream, nonfat
1 cup yogurt, nonfat plain
1 cup salsa

Instructions:

1. Mix the sour cream, yogurt, and salsa.

2. Store the dip in a covered container if you don't plan to eat it right away.

3. Keep the dip in the refrigerator until you serve it.

Note: Serve with baked tortilla chips, crackers, or bite-sized vegetables.

Per serving: 25 calories, 0 g fat, 1 g protein, 5 g carbohydrate, 5 mg cholesterol, 85 mg sodium

Cost: Per Recipe: $ 2.57; Per Serving: $ 0.16

Fresh Salsa

Serving Size: 1/2 cup
Yield: 4 servings

Ingredients:

2 chopped tomatoes
1/2 chopped onion
3 finely chopped, seeded if desired, jalapeño chilies
1/4 cup chopped cilantro
1/4 teaspoon salt
1 juiced lime

Instructions:

1. In a medium bowl, mix all ingredients.

2. Serve or store salsa in refrigerator for up to three days in a covered plastic or glass container.

Safety Tip: Caution: When handling hot peppers, the oils can cause burning and skin irritation. You can wear clean kitchen gloves or wash hands thoroughly after preparing. KEEP HANDS AWAY FROM EYES.

Per serving: 30 calories, 0 g fat, 1 g protein, 6 g carbohydrate, 0 mg cholesterol, 150 mg sodium

Cost: Per Recipe: $ 1.37; Per Serving: $ 0.34

Melon Salsa

Serving Size: 1/4 cup
Yield: 12 servings

Ingredients:

2 cups seeded and chopped fresh melon, honeydew, cantaloupe or watermelon, (use one kind or a combination)
1 cup peeled, seeded and chopped cucumber
1/4 cup chopped onion, red or white
2 Tablespoons fresh, chopped cilantro or mint (optional)
1/2 - 1 seeded and finely chopped jalapeño or hot sauce to taste
1/4 cup lime juice or lemon juice
1 Tablespoon sugar, white or brown

Instructions:

1. In a medium size bowl, stir together all ingredients.

2. Taste and season with more lemon or lime juice, sugar if needed.

3. Cover and chill for at least 30 minutes. Serve with grilled or broiled fish or chicken.

Safety Tip: Caution: When handling hot peppers, the oils can cause burning and skin irritation. You can wear clean kitchen gloves or wash hands thoroughly after preparing. KEEP HANDS AWAY FROM EYES.

Per serving: 15 calories, 0 g fat, 0 g protein, 4 g carbohydrate, 0 mg cholesterol, 0 mg sodium

Cost: Per Recipe: $ 1.55; Per Serving: $ 0.13

INDEX

Printed in the United Kingdom by
Lightning Source UK Ltd., Milton Keynes
139559UK00002B/37/P